MISTAKE-FREE
GOLF

MISTAKE-FREE GOLF

First Aid for Your Golfing Brain

Robert K. Winters, Ph.D.

Foreword by Rich Lerner

ST. MARTIN'S PRESS ❦ NEW YORK

MISTAKE-FREE GOLF. Copyright © 2014 by Robert K. Winters, Ph.D. Foreword copyright © 2014 by Rich Lerner. All rights reserved. Printed in the United States of America. For information, address St. Martin's Press, 175 Fifth Avenue, New York, N.Y. 10010.

www.stmartins.com

Designed by Steven Seighman

The Library of Congress Cataloging-in-Publication Data
is available upon request.

ISBN 978-1-250-04468-6 (hardcover)
ISBN 978-1-4668-4315-8 (e-book)

St. Martin's Press books may be purchased for educational, business, or promotional use. For information on bulk purchases, please contact Macmillan Corporate and Premium Sales Department at 1-800-221-7945, extension 5442, or write specialmarkets@macmillan.com.

First Edition: May 2014

10 9 8 7 6 5 4 3 2 1

I dedicate this book to my former collegiate coach at Ball State University, the late Earl Yestingsmeier, and to my great friend Dr. Herbert Price of Logansport, Indiana. Both of these wonderful people believed in me and gave me a chance to know that by making a few mistakes along the way and learning from those failings helps create the pathways for future growth and success. I will always be grateful for the life lessons you helped me learn along the way.

CONTENTS

FOREWORD

The great Bobby Jones famously once said, "Competitive golf is played mainly on a five-and-a-half-inch course—the space between your ears." Jones was both talented and wise. It's the head that matters most. I've always been labeled a monumental head case going back to my days as a young golfer of mild promise at my father's driving range in Pennsylvania. And to this day, I'm often still too technical, too judgmental, and too unreasonable with my expectations.

Mistake-Free Golf is as essential to skillfully navigating those five and a half inches as Calamity Jane was to Jones's unparalleled success in the 1920s. I've known Dr. Bob Winters for better than a decade through my work at Golf Channel. More personally, he's been a fixture at an annual charity event organized by my family in Orlando.

Dr. Bob has spent a lifetime trying to unlock the answers to why we seem to limit ourselves with negative thinking. He delves into such areas as status anxiety, commitment, as well as indecision and doubt. And he shares his case studies with the likes of Hall of Fame great Nick Price and LPGA standout Suzann Pettersen. You might be surprised to learn that while their physical talents are otherworldly, the psychological challenges they face are not that much different from the ones facing golfers of every level.

What I love about *Mistake-Free Golf* is that it's highly practical, easy to read and understand, and best of all you can take Dr. Bob's remedies right to the golf course.

You'll feel better about your game and better about yourself. And who among us hasn't linked those two areas, golf and life? Mark O'Meara once joked with me that on his way to winning the 1998 Masters he'd hit a poor iron shot and was really down, silently berating himself as not just a bad golfer but a bad human being.

If you've ever been there, and Lord knows I have, if you've ever wondered what it's like to play this game with freedom and peace of mind, then I urge you to read the good doctor's recommendations. *Mistake-Free Golf* may be the single best and most economically sensible investment you've ever made in your golfing life!

—Rich Lerner,
Golf Channel

PROLOGUE

The Greatest Lesson Ever Learned

Anyone who has never made a mistake
has never tried anything new.
—ALBERT EINSTEIN

People who play golf often comment that a sport psychologist must have the best job in the world. That is, as a mental coach, you may spend a good deal of your time working and consulting with some of the best players and golf teachers on the planet. You may also get the chance now and then to play fabulous courses with great athletes who are always picking your brain to help them with theirs. What many of these folks (who, by the way, just happen to notice that the grass is always greener on the other side of the fence) fail to realize is that it takes a great deal of time and personal investment to help harness change with another human being.

Consider yourself for a moment and stop and reflect about how you react to something new or different. Do you like it? Most people don't. People tend to resist change. If something is unfamiliar and feels uncomfortable, it is human nature to resist the implementation of change. Or, if a philosophy or a style of play that you learned from a young age is different from the one being presented, change becomes even harder. Now you are starting to understand the challenge a mental coach must deal with every day. Mental and emotional training is just as exhausting and frustrating to develop as it is to create and maintain a great swing. Perhaps the mental game is even harder because obtaining an EEG or MRI of a poor thought pattern is not as accessible as filming a golf swing! The quest to find the core answer with a golfer is a bit like being a detective. You have to uncover all of the clues in order to render a judgment and then prescribe an effective treatment.

This means that a careful analysis for each and every athlete is a crucial and delicate situation. (And make no mistake about it, if you are a golfer, you are an athlete.) The words that you use and the interventions that you provide must make sense and be simple for your athletes to implement. If I cannot communicate something correctly or if I don't make a connection with my athlete, then I am ineffective and I fail. Athletes rarely give a sport psychologist a second chance if he or she is not effective. Positive **results** for your athletes, not positive intent, are crucial to your success.

But people are absolutely right. A sport psychologist does have a great job, and I thank my lucky stars every day that I get the chance to listen to and interact with some of the best athletes in the world. The gratification that comes from watching your work turn into athletic reality in the achievement of personal goals and long-held dreams is quite special. Through my association with media outlets such as Golf Channel, ESPN, and CBS Sports, *Golfweek* and *Golf Fitness Magazine*, I have been able to spread my message of sport psychology to a great many people around the globe, for which I am extremely grateful.

Although I do much of my professional consulting as the resident sport psychologist for the Leadbetter Golf Academy World Headquarters at an exquisite resort known as ChampionsGate (which is just down the road from Disney World), I personally belong to a wonderful golf club in central Orlando known as Orange Tree Golf Club. Orange Tree is a haven for aspiring tour players and also possesses strong playing memberships in both the men's and women's golf associations. It is just a couple of blocks from Arnold Palmer's Bay Hill Club and the Isleworth Club, which is the home of many PGA tour professionals and is perhaps best known as where Tiger Woods lived for many years before his infamous accident with a fire hydrant that created a media frenzy and a change in his personal and professional life.

Orange Tree Golf Club is widely known in the Orlando community as the tightest course in the area. Although it may not have the glamour or prestige of a Bay Hill or Isleworth, the Orange Tree layout tests your ability on every club in the bag, and if you can play Orange Tree, you can pretty much play anywhere in the world.

One of the unique features at Orange Tree is a seventy-eight-year-old member who can be found either on the driving range working on his game or sitting in the clubhouse dispensing his golfing wisdom. His name is Walter Zembriski, and he is a former PGA and Senior PGA Tour winner. He is perhaps the one player who truly fits the "anything's possible" PGA marketing tagline. Walter, or, as he is known to his friends, the Z Man, is a reflection of the players who never considered mental training a viable option because, in their time, they didn't have access to sport psychologists and focusing on the mental game wasn't considered part of golf. The great Ben Hogan had spoken of "digging his secret out of the dirt," and the golfers of that era and the following twenty years pretty much adhered to that philosophy.

Every veteran golfer of this era knew that the mind was important, but the players didn't take the time to work on their mental games as much as they perhaps needed to and opted instead to hit balls and develop their confidence that way. For them, the secret was truly in the ground, and the only way to learn the secret was to pound the ball and turn over a bit more of the green sod. However, in my discussions with many tour veterans over the years, almost to a person each of them acknowledged that they knew their mental attitude was vital to their success, but they never spoke of it outwardly because they didn't want to give any of their secrets away. They always wanted to have an edge.

When I first approached Walter on this project, I knew of his history on the PGA and Senior Tours and that he had won the New Jersey Amateur and several regional professional tournaments. I also knew that he was tough-minded and had grown up with a strong work ethic as an ironworker who spent years doing hard labor in the construction industry. When I told him of the focus of the book, he seemed interested and we continued to talk. I asked him point-blank, "Z, what is the single greatest mental mistake that plagued you during your career?" He responded:

"Hell, I never even thought about that stuff. I never thought about mental mistakes. In fact, I've never had a sports psychologist! I just went out and played. I had good days and bad days but I never really thought about some of the stuff that you guys are talking about now. Heck, I never worried about a mental mistake; I just tried to get the ball in the hole as fast as I could."

Walter paused to ponder his words, then continued:

"Yeah, I have played with the best of them, Arnie, Jack, Hale, and everybody else. It didn't matter to me who I was playing with. . . . I knew that I had to take care of me and that was it."

I was intrigued, and Walter then discussed an important golf lesson that altered his entire philosophy about the game . . . perhaps without his even realizing it until I brought it up. When Walter was a young teenager, he had a conversation with his father and learned a golf lesson that wasn't about the grip or the stance but one of the heart and the mind.

WALTER'S FIRST AND MOST IMPORTANT MENTAL GAME LESSON

When Walter was a fourteen-year-old golfer playing in New Jersey, he entered a large regional golf tournament named after one of the largest newspapers in the area, the Journal American Golf Classic. All of the region's best young players were going to be playing. Walter went to the course to practice, looked up and down the line of his fellow competitors, and saw a number of local and regional "hotshots." He practiced that day but returned home doubting whether he could play with some of these "name" players. He knew that the next day he was going to be in the same group as a player with a reputation as one of the state's best junior golfers.

The evening before the first round, Walter's father, Stanley Zembriski, noticed that his son was talking about the tournament and kept mentioning that he had to play with some of the best golfers in the area. Seeing Walt's uneasiness, Stanley made a bold statement. Stanley told Walter that if he was thinking about the other players and getting nervous about being paired with them, he didn't need to be playing at all! He might as well take his clubs and put them away because they wouldn't do him any good since his mind was so poorly focused. Stanley's advice helped Walter realize that if you are worried about what the other guys are doing, or you are questioning your talent or ability, then you shouldn't even bother to play because you are already defeated before you hit your first tee shot!

Stanley Zembriski did not have a degree in sport psychology, but he knew something about "name" players and intimidating personalities and how to deal with them effectively. Years earlier, Stanley had been a caddie for the legendary New York Yankee slugger Babe Ruth. Stanley knew how intimidating it could be when someone was paired with the "Sultan of Swat." Playing with "the Babe" could be overwhelming for the unsuspecting golfer. So, after listening to Walter go on about his competition, Stanley said, "Walter, if you are scared of a name or someone's reputation, then don't even bother to go play. You might as well just take your clubs and put them in the cellar right now!" Stanley's intention was to encourage Walter to believe in his talent and give himself permission to play his own game and dismiss the other players from his mind. Stanley Zembriski was teaching a vital life lesson:

A name or reputation never beat anyone . . . *unless* you allow that name or reputation to intimidate you and affect your play. If you give in to the name and reputation in a negative way, you are giving away your personal power. You are giving away your most valuable asset: *your belief in yourself.*

Letting go of others and believing that you have the tools to successfully compete is what this early life lesson was all about.

By stating his point bluntly, Stanley was giving Walter the impetus to focus on what he needed to do without worrying about others. In essence, he was getting Walter to play the game of golf versus playing the game of comparing oneself to others.

Walter's response to my initial question about mental mistakes, "I never even thought about that stuff," may have been Walter's way of suppressing the fear of failing and dismissing the doubt. By listening to his father's sage advice and believing in his talent (and letting go of others), Walter learned a lesson that worked successfully for the former ironworker for a number of years as a member of the PGA Senior Tour. Walter had a solid career, earning over $3 million dollars and scoring victories over many Hall of Fame golfers.

When I heard from Walter's mouth this valuable lesson he received from his father, I wondered, Does Walter know the value that this mental lesson had for his career? Does he appreciate what the lesson was about? We may never know. What is truly ironic and great about the Walter Zembriski story is that he received the greatest lesson in mental golf training that one can learn . . . and he probably didn't even recognize it at the time!

INTRODUCTION

No One Is Immune

*The difference between greatness and mediocrity is
often how an individual views a mistake.*

—NELSON BOSWELL

Let's face it: golf can be a simple game one day and a struggle the
next. You never know which type of day is going to show up or
even which type of golfer you will be. It is when a golfer says, "I
don't know who is going to show up today. . . . I don't know if I
am going to play like a champion or play like a chump!" The
uncertainty of what can unfold is one of the fascinating aspects
why millions of golfers play this crazy and wonderful game.

Golf is a game of managing your misses and maximizing your
less than perfect shots. Golf is a blend of hitting great and poor
shots and trying your best to get the ball into the hole as fast as
you can. Even when you don't have your best stuff, it's always
satisfying to know that you still have the opportunity to score
well and have a great time getting the ball into the hole. But
golf is also about making poor swings and creating mistakes
that lead to big numbers and a bruised ego. From the number

of golfers that I have worked with through the years, it seems the latter statement is more common than the first. That is what this book is about. It is about recognizing and identifying your golfing mistakes and how to correct your thinking and behavior so that you will avoid making them.

You may think it illogical to have a book on making mistakes because one of the things that we try to avoid is making a mental blunder. Most mental-help books talk about being focused and expound on the benefits of positive thinking. They provide adequate descriptions of the type of golfer that one desires to be, but they fail to tell you *how* to correct your misdirected thinking. As a human, you will make mental errors of omission and commission. Whether you want to or not, you will screw up. This book is about helping you to avoid mental errors on the golf course and to have the ability to recognize when you are not thinking clearly and to get yourself into a better frame of mind. You will learn how to take action so that you can *do* something to create better golf shots. The key is getting you to think and behave effectively so that you can break through the chains of your self-created fears and doubts, rather than just talk and worry about them.

Let's examine this issue using a different perspective. In this age of preventive and corrective medicine, we are bombarded with healthy alternatives and solutions to help us think clearer, act more responsibly, and be in overall better mental and physical health. Those people who are truly interested in a longer and more productive life are motivated to act and reap the benefits from these lifestyle changes.

However, most people do not take the initiative or any action until they need medical help. People wait until they become sick or need treatment before they seek medical attention. At this point they need corrective or surgical procedures to bring them back to better health. A sad truth is that most people have to be scared or come close to suffering a major illness before they change their behavior to a healthier life style. And for some, even that is not enough, until it is too late. This book was written because millions of golfers suffer from mental golf mistakes and performance illness. They need a cure to bring them back to proper golfing health. The affliction of a misdirected focus leads to inappropriate action and takes its toll on your golfing performance. This is a "treatment" book that provides specific methods and strategies to help you be your own doctor of mental golf health. When you utilize these strategies, you separate yourself from the majority of golfers, who make the same mistakes repeatedly, and have a self-help guide to great golf. This is a first-aid book for your golf mind! To illustrate my points, I first describe the ailment and then discuss Dr. Bob's Rx for Success treatment. In this way, you not only cure your ailment, but learn how to prevent it from happening again.

For far too long we have been exposed to simplistic and banal views of the mental game. Many of the books that have been written focus on the typical menu of mental golf strategies: goal setting, visualization, preshot-routine compliance, and a sprinkling of course and self-management. We have all been exposed to the phrases of golf newscasters and quick-help mental gurus, such as "stay in the moment," "be the ball," "play one shot at a time," and "get into your happy place." Many books have no answers to cure or eliminate mental clutter because they fail to look at the root of the problem and focus too much on the symptoms.

The previous phrases are similar to the ones that I use every day in my work, but when I converse with my players, I want them to fully understand these words. I want them to know what a phrase such as "being in the moment" is truly about and create a "feeling of owning" that moment. We work hard to develop an understanding of what key words or phrases mean when they speak their "golf talk" in relation to the images, thoughts, and feelings that they produce when they are playing on the course. Then and only then are we speaking "apples to apples" and conversing in a language that we both understand because they are conveying their innermost thoughts and feelings in a specific word form that means something to them. Anything less than that type of communication can only lead to ambiguous awareness and performance failure.

For example, it doesn't do any good to tell a player who is having a panic attack on the first tee, "Relax," any more than to tell a drowning victim, "Swim!" It doesn't work because people do not have the correction skills to implement in the time of crisis. When you are on the golf course and find yourself ready to throw up because of fear of your shot, it is a poor strategy to tell yourself to be confident and "just get through it." You will always find a way to sabotage your talent and bring your horrific past into the present and screw up! It also doesn't do much good for someone on the sidelines to be analyzing your struggle and watching you drown in your mental dilemma and then to describe the water as being wet. You don't need a description; you need a prescription for treading water and staying afloat!

As a golfer who wants to improve, you make errors of judgment and indecision during play. You will more than likely make a few mental, physical, and sensory errors. Like many of the millions of golfers that play regularly, you may try so hard to avoid screwing up that you get in your own way and end up making an error anyway! The problem is that golfers fail to realize that they are overtrying. An errorproof round is quite unusual. So, the key is to create an awareness of your problem areas and eliminate as many of your self-created mistakes as possible.

If you say that you don't make many of these mistakes, you are probably lying to yourself, but that is not my point. The point is that if you intend to play great, unforced errors of mental judgment will show up. Even the greats of golf such as Ben Hogan, Arnold Palmer, Jack Nicklaus, Nancy Lopez, and Annika Sörenstam made mental faux pas in their careers. The good news is that each of these players learned to identify and self-correct their mental thorns (or minimized their occurrence) and played on to become fantastic sports heroes and legends.

No one is immune from the effects of a wayward or misdirected mind. Not me . . . not you . . . not anyone! One of golf's aspects universal to everyone who plays is that we all make the same or similar errors. Not even our era's greatest players, such as Tiger Woods, Phil Mickelson, or Suzann Pettersen, are free from every psychological land mine. Even Tiger has repeatedly stated that a golfer should never make a mental mistake because the ball is just sitting there, waiting for you to act upon it.

What this means is that because golf is a proactive sport (meaning that we act upon the situation and make the action happen . . . rather than a reactive sport such as tennis, in which the ball is moving and we have to respond to it), we have virtually all of the time in the world before we make our swing to initiate the correct procedure. But we still go ahead and make the unforced or unwanted mental error. Even Tiger has admitted to making a mental error or two along the way, and he is one of golf's all-time best, *if not the best,* at getting his mind in the proper place before he steps into the ball. So, if Tiger can admit to making a mental error now and then, you shouldn't feel so bad about admitting that you could probably do better in this area as well.

The core idea of this book is to help you play better golf through your own insight . . . or rather your own personal awareness. That is where you have to start. Personal awareness is understanding how you think and what you are thinking about *and then* to be able to identify your mental weaknesses. By recognizing your weaknesses and knowing that they can be modified, you can make yourself stronger. It is much like being aware that you are not feeling well and taking a trip to the doctor's office. You meet with your doctor and describe your symptoms. After you have been diagnosed, the doctor prescribes a remedy for your ailment. In golf, I want you to be your own doctor and also your best patient. The simple cure for your mental affliction starts with your awareness that your mind and attitude are not where you need them to be and that you have the insight to recognize the warning symptoms and take appropriate steps to correct them.

The statements, interviews, and examples throughout this book all come from real golfers. The information was obtained by me informally during the past six years, and the insights and responses were all generated from a single question about mental errors. I simply went up to the best players of the game (or the most emotionally challenged players in the game) and asked, "What is the greatest mental mistake that has plagued you during your career?" The people on my list are quite impressive and include an eclectic combination of touring professionals, coaches, teaching professionals, and collegiate and amateur players. Many of the touring professionals are living legends and Hall of Fame golfers. But all of the golfers that I questioned were kind enough to share the innermost thoughts that have boggled their minds during their careers, and a few shared ideas about how they tried to correct them.

What I found fascinating during the questioning was that

almost to a person, players were extremely animated in their discussion of mental mistakes. It seemed that for most of them, the chance to discuss their primary mistake was cathartic, and many were surprised (and perhaps even a bit relieved) that players of great repute and fame had faced the same or similar issues.

For others, the mental demons still remain and come back and haunt them from time to time. But with this wealth of insight and information, I will help you become aware of the many different types of mental errors that golfers frequently encounter and how to recognize and correct each of them. I want to simplify the way that you play your game, not to make it any tougher than it already is.

My intention in each chapter is to identify a common mental mistake with several player examples, focus on it, describe the mental dilemma, and then prescribe a solution. You can take this information directly to the golf course and apply it. You will have the power to self-correct any mistake you make on the course and play with confidence. More confidence and greater self-control lead to lower scores.

In chapter 1, "I Don't Believe in Myself" I present the most common mental mistake, and in each subsequent chapter I discuss mental issues and present personal interviews and statements by leading golfers who have experienced the issue firsthand. I describe the problem ("The Mental Mistake") and prescribe an intervention strategy ("Dr. Bob's Rx for Success") to correct the situation. Also, at the end of each chapter I have provided a segment labeled "Take It to the Course," which reinforces the key elements of the lessons within the chapter. In this way, you will be reminded several times of the key aspects of how to correct the problem when you go to the course! Repetition and good-habit formation is what makes a great golf swing, and it also builds a strong mental foundation as well!

A quotation at the start of each chapter, from some of the most revered philosophers, thinkers, and influential members of our world society, focuses on mistakes. Many of these quotes are from people who left this earth a long time ago, but their sage advice forges on. The lessons we learn from our golf mistakes are the foundation for success both on and off the course.

Eliminating your mental mistakes is what this book is about. It is a guide to help you correct your mental deficiencies and to remove the doubt and fear that you suffer in tournament competition or simply when you are playing in your favorite foursome. Imagine playing your next round of golf with a mind-set that is clear from distraction and doubt and also changes your perception of pressure situations so that they appear as ones you handle well—a mind-set that is comparable to that of the greatest players of all time.

So, are you ready to play the most error-free golf of your life? The information that follows after this page is your first step to insure that it is done. The choice is yours. Begin your journey with me now and learn how to create a mind-set of positivity and decisiveness versus a mind-set that is weak and yields to inner and external pressures. You will find that the answers to many of these problems are transferable to every other area of your life. After reading the text, I hope that you play your next round with a heightened sense of mental and emotional freedom. Enjoy the read and the ride! It is definitely worth the price of the ticket.

ONE

I Don't Believe in Myself

*The greatest mistake you can make in life
is to be continually fearing you will make one.*
—Elbert Hubbard

LIGHTS . . . CAMERA . . . ANXIETY!

Here is the situation: You are on the practice tee and a large group of reporters and camera crews from ESPN, Fox Sports, and Golf Channel show up with their lights and cameras to film and interview *you*! What would you think? You may be asking yourself, Why do they want to film me? Is this a joke or some sort of golf reality show? Then, what if one of the sportscasters puts a microphone in front of your face and asks, "Are you mentally strong?" How would you reply? Would you look directly into the camera and say, "Yes, absolutely!" Or would you be more reserved and hesitant? Would you need a bit of time to think it over before you gave your answer? What if they asked the question in a different way: "Do you ever make mental mistakes when you play golf?" Now what would your answer be?

If you replied to the first question that you are mentally strong, then good for you. Having a self-concept that brims with self-confidence is vital to playing consistently well. But the majority of us tend to be a bit more restrained in our estimation of our golf worth. It's not that we don't value our talent, but we know firsthand that golf is a tough game to play in general and especially at a high level of consistency. Humility tends to be learned on the course via the school of hard knocks and unexpected results. So, our guttural response is going to be a bit guarded due to the challenging nature of the game itself.

However, in response to the second question, many of us fess up and admit to making mental errors. We all realize that in our golfing lives we are not bulletproof or invincible. We have all asked ourselves when playing the best round of our lives, Will I be able to close the deal? Will I be able to hang on and finish well? Is today the day that I succeed? These questions of doubt and suspicion rule our innermost thoughts and desires. We have all faced these demons, and sometimes we succeed and other times we fail. But when we fail, the fallout from the emotional devastation is more lasting on our psyches than the joys of the minor victories.

Let me ask you one more question: How many times have you said to yourself "that was stupid" or "I just wasn't into it" or "I just knew that was going to happen" immediately after a poor shot? (Think about that one for a minute.) The point I am trying to make is, if you could eliminate every mental mistake or hesitation in your golfing round that led to a shot below your ability, how much better could you be? I imagine you would say much better! That is what playing mentally strong golf is all about. It is about stepping into your shot with the freedom to swing with trust and know that your ball is going to your intended target!

THE GREATEST INTERFERENCE: SELF-DOUBT

Many golfers that I have counseled over the years have told me that when they are over the ball, they feel doubt and anxiety. They are worried that they will hit a poor shot, embarrass themselves, or that others are judging them. They become "self-aware" rather than "target-aware." That is, their mind is focused on past poor performance rather than on where it needs to be . . . the target. These players become so immersed in their thoughts that they fail to trust their talent and second-guess their decisions. They start to hit poor shots and eventually lose confidence in themselves. These internal issues are directly linked to the mind-body connection of how thoughts affect feelings and vice versa. Even if your feelings or thoughts are unfounded, the fallout from them remains the same and creates ineffective shots and results.

The greatest interference that you will have in your life is not negative evaluation from others, but your self-doubt. Your doubt and the incessant worry about your ability to play the way that you expect is the greatest roadblock to your golfing success. More important, every mental mistake you make is woven directly into the doubt and fear that you carry into every shot you play. In discussing doubt and mental mistakes with golfers of all levels for this book, I often found mixed feelings about how a player interprets success, confidence, and failure. It seems all golfers have their own story to tell, and when discussing doubt and fear, they feel as if they are the only ones that feel this way.

Part of the odd nature of golf is that it often creates feelings of doubt and uncertainty about one's abilities *even when those talents have been honed to precision over years of practice and competition.* Despite knowing that doubt and indecision affect their behavior, many golfers with multiple years of experience still struggle with doubt and an inability to believe that good things will happen. They worry that bad events will happen, and they eventually sabotage their talent. They end up second-guessing themselves and before long they become mentally frustrated and lose confidence. Thus we have a multitude of golfers who stymie themselves with self-limiting thoughts and feelings even before they step onto the first tee.

There are as many error-producing thoughts and worries that plague golfers as there are players of this vexing game. Many of these thoughts are of failure, anxiety, and the inability to pull off a certain shot in a particular situation. Worries about whether other players will respect your swing or even acknowledge you as a good player affect your self-image and self-confidence. The following section highlights but a few of the mental errors that established players of every faction of professional and amateur golf suffer. As you read these passages, you may find yourself immersed in their words and suffering from the same calamity.

MENTAL ERROR REVELATIONS

Here are a few excerpts from some of the touring professionals and top teachers who were kind enough to share their experiences of doubt. The first is from Cameron Yancey, a young touring professional whom I coached at the University of Virginia during the 1990s. Cameron was the first player to graduate from the University of Virginia and qualify to play on the PGA Tour. Cameron discusses the frustration of losing himself when he was on tour and finding that his self-doubt and the expectations of others reinforced his concerns about his ability to play at golf's highest level.

THE MENTAL MISTAKE #1

My biggest mental mistake is not staying true to myself and believing in my talent. In my rookie year on the PGA Tour, I guess I was just unprepared for the stargazing that went on and I got out of my comfort zone and got away from being Cameron Yancey. I guess I just lost my own game and was trying to be someone else, and when you do that, you are done.

Also, when I would miss a cut, it seemed that everyone is coming up to you and asking you what is wrong and you need to be doing this and doing that, and before long, your confidence is shot and you start to question your ability to play. It's as if you miss a couple of cuts and you can't play anymore, and I don't know if anyone else feels like that, but that's what I felt like. I mean my confidence would be shaken and then I would start trying different things and I got away from doing the things that I normally do that got me on the PGA Tour in the first place!

So, my mental mistake is not being me and trying to be someone else. For example, I normally draw the ball and I can control it very well. Well, when I got to the tour, there was just player after player who said, "You need to learn how to cut it. If you don't learn how to fade the ball, you will be done in no time." Well, I listened to those guys and what happened? I screwed myself up and lost the confidence in my playing ability because I was trying to hit the ball like everyone else and I am not like anyone else. I am Cameron Yancey and I need to play like Cameron Yancey.

DR. BOB'S Rx FOR SUCCESS

Just like Cameron, many of us have a game that works well for us and brings us success. However, in trying to improve and get better, we immerse ourselves in new training procedures and abandon what it is that we do well. We start searching for other ways to do the things that we have done well, and by virtue of experimentation we end up losing ourselves and our game. In Cameron's case, his belief in his game and what he could do with the golf ball is what earned him the chance to play on the PGA Tour in the first place! However, Cameron was seduced by many of the common mental dilemmas that often face young players who are not familiar with or are unable to recognize mental mistakes when they appear.

The first mental mistake that Cameron committed was the "stargazing" when he first arrived on the PGA Tour. This is a very human yet overwhelming mental mistake. When you place more focus on the people around you than on taking care of number one (which is you), your concentration is off and can only lead to poor performance. One can only imagine walking onto the practice tee alongside the likes of Tiger, Phil, and Paula and knowing that you are now among players whom you had only before seen on your flat-screen TV. Talk about being out of your comfort zone!

This is similar to what many of us go through when we play in our local tournaments or even when we have our weekend skins game with a couple of new players. We size up our competition. We start to wonder, Do I have the ability to compete with these other players? This self-reflection often leads to speculation and doubt. Much like Walter Zembriski, Cameron needed to let go of the other players and remind himself that he had the game to compete . . . otherwise he wouldn't have gotten on the tour in the first place!

Dr. Bob's Rx for Success is basic: Let go of all those around you because you cannot control their games, nor can they control yours. You must understand that your game . . . is your game . . . and no one else can play or think like you. The golf course and the challenge of the game is your true opponent, not the other players! So, the next time you go out to play, play the golf course with the game you have and let the name players do their thing and you will have a much better day on the course.

The next mistake that created doubt is that Cameron listened to the well-intended advice of other players; he got away from being true to himself and the way that he played. He wasn't playing Cameron Yancey golf. He talked about how other players insisted that he needed to fade the ball rather than draw the ball, which was his dominant and "go to" shot. Allowing others to influence his thinking and basic beliefs about his game created doubts that sent Cameron on a search mission to find something else that might work even better than what he already had. But what happened isn't what Cameron intended at all; it only heightened the problem.

Think about what Cameron experienced and put yourself in his shoes. If everyone around you is asking, "What's wrong with you? Why aren't you playing well?," how would you react? If all that is being said to you creates a question mark in your mind and is constantly being hammered into your head . . . eventually you will start to doubt yourself and begin looking into the mirror and asking, What is wrong with *me*?

What Cameron learned from this experience is the ultimate

life lesson we must all learn: we are individuals. No one else on this golfing planet is the same or thinks the same as ourself. We must disallow the good intentions of others and stay true to our gut instincts and do our own thing. In trying to be perfect or to play like other golfers, we often give up our personal genius and end up losing ourselves and our self-confidence. As the old saying goes, "no one is more qualified at being you . . . than you!"

I am not saying that self-improvement and searching for excellence is a bad thing, because we are all striving to improve our technical, mental, and physical abilities in golf. But when you alter or make compromises that interfere with the innate and developed talents that have taken you to a high level, then you must assess thoroughly if change is warranted. The Cameron Yancey story is vital to understanding that to be truly self-confident, you must assess your talent, believe in yourself, and learn to dismiss the good intentions of others who want you to change and be untrue to your real self. Remember, all that you have is yourself, but that should be more than enough if you truly believe in your ability.

THE MENTAL MISTAKE #2

The second example of the mental mistake of doubt and a poor belief system comes from South African Deanne Pappas. Sometimes our most egregious golfing mistakes come about from lost opportunities or having failed in the past. The emotional fallout from these miscues causes us to worry whenever we face similar situations again. Deanne faces his greatest mental challenge on the putting green:

I guess my biggest mental mistake would have to be that I question my ability to be a good putter, and I know that over the years I have had a lot of success. It is a funny thing, but I am over the putt now and I am thinking after I hit a good putt and the ball is halfway to the hole, I am talking to myself and saying, "How am I going to get screwed out of this one!" Now what is that all about?

I don't know how I got to this position in my career, but I know that I have a good stroke because everyone tells me, "Wow, you have such a good stroke and the ball rolls so well," but I think . . . if that is true, how come I am always missing the putt? I make great rolls but the ball doesn't go into the hole. It just becomes so frustrating after a while and it wears your confidence in putting way down.

DR. BOB'S Rx FOR SUCCESS

Worry and doubt seem most clearly evidenced in golf on the putting green. This is because putting is black-and-white. Either you make the putt or you miss. The golf ball does not discriminate nor does it play favorites. The golf ball does not care how much you want to make the putt or how scared you are of missing. You cannot hide from your lack of belief in your putting ability because the ball will not lie. It only goes where your mind is focusing. If you fear missing, then that is what you create in your mind, and your body will respond to that directive. Hence, you putt and you miss. If you feel confident and self-assured that you can putt well, you will hit your putt solidly and it has a good chance to go in.

From his statements, Deanne is making the mental mistake of sabotaging his success even before his ball has finished rolling! Deanne may not perceive it, but through the years he has perhaps talked himself into the habit of reacting negatively to his putting. By instantly reacting to the feel of the putt before it finishes, he dismisses all of the positive memories from years past and the affirmations that he has received from people who tell him that he has a great stroke.

Interestingly, he has a history of success on the greens, but *even with his success, he is still finding ways to undermine his belief that he is a good putter!* This situation needs a fix and fast! If you share Deanne's problem, then here are two things that you need to do:

1. First, you need to suspend evaluation and judgment by the result. That is, you need to develop the philosophy that a putt is not good or bad because of the result, but should be judged by your overall commitment to and execution of the stroke of the ball. You must place more emphasis on your commitment to your read and to the execution of a good stroke than whether the ball goes in the hole. When you place too much value on whether the ball goes in the hole, you have created "must" thinking. You feel that you "must" make the putt and nothing else is more important. The focus of "must" makes it simply all or nothing on the green. If you make your putt, then all is well with the world. That is the way it is supposed to be.

   However, if you miss, then you are an awful putter or you hit a crappy putt. This type of distorted thinking is perhaps what has led Deanne to second-guess himself on the greens. All-or-nothing thinking, the "must" mind-set, places too much pressure on the performer. The sooner you can get into your routine and trust your putting process, the sooner you will start to sink more putts.

2. The second thing that Deanne can do is create positive self-talk. That is, after a putt or shot comes to a stop, instead of beating himself up because the results weren't what he wanted or expected, he can say something good to himself. By saying something positive after the ball is hit, he can direct his energy into the effectiveness of the process rather than into worry about the result. For example, if Deanne left his putt short but it was dead center toward the hole, he can say to himself, "That was just one roll shy of perfection. I hit the ball exactly where I wanted to hit it and my routine was flowing." By doing this, he is focusing on the good aspects of his putting procedure versus focusing on results.

Deanne's statements make it quite clear that his self-talk was not helping him. Until he stops the negative self-talk, he will never be the confident putter that everyone else sees in him. Confidence is hard to achieve if you are always knocking yourself down. If you are guilty of being too hard on yourself, then I suggest you stop negative self-talk and replace it with positive suggestions about things that you can control. Accept that you are too critical and negative and change into a more effective and positive mind-set. The two items suggested above will work wonders for your putting success.

THE MENTAL MISTAKE #3

Sometimes our failure to believe in ourselves happens when we least expect it. Our next example of a mental mistake comes from LPGA touring professional and college golf coach Ashley Prange. Ashley is a tenacious competitor and was the winner of Golf Channel's *Big Break V: Hawaii*. Ashley speaks of having doubt and questioning her ability when she addresses the ball:

> My biggest mental mistake is just having a lot of doubt and questioning my ability when I am standing over the ball. I have all of these thoughts about "Where am I aimed? Am I on target, or am I too far right or left?" It is so frustrating to play the game of golf as long as I have and to still have so many thoughts that lead me to mistrust my ability and create tension in my swing. When I get clear about my plan and my shot, that tends to help me free it up a little bit and I can swing with more trust to my target, but I have always tended to have a bit of doubt. But, I am working very hard on moving through all of the mental distractions that seem to plague everybody at one time or another.

DR. BOB'S Rx FOR SUCCESS

Knowing that your body is aimed correctly is a major issue in building movement confidence. Movement confidence is a specific form of physical confidence in which you feel effective in a dynamic situation. Ashley talks of her frustration because she feels that she shouldn't have this issue after having played the game for as long as she has. Being over the ball and having doubt is no way to think because it creates tension. Tension is a killer of rhythm, tempo, and fluidity. Here is the cure.

1. If you have doubt while standing over the ball in the address position, you need to develop a more comprehensive plan of action. You must assess the situation, analyze all of your options, and make a clear decision about what shot you want to hit. This decision should be made *behind the ball* and *before* you make your first step to the ball. Making absolutely sure that you have thought the situation through and you have a positive action plan for executing a shot will create a feeling of assurance and trust. This feeling will transfer into your having a greater rhythm while you are executing your swing.

2. Second, away from the course, practice your setup and address position. Place clubs or use chalk or paint lines on the ground to give you precise feedback as to the placement of your feet and how your shoulders, hips, and body align to your feet. Rehearsing and knowing that you are well aimed will eliminate a lot of stress when you head to the golf course to play. Preparation and readiness are key elements to building trust and confidence.

3. Third, have a friend or your teacher give you feedback on the practice range and also on the course. With feedback from another pair of eyes, you can instantly get yourself set up properly and learn from that setup.

4. Finally, when you step into the ball, focus on the target and not on yourself or your setup. Your setup should be automatic and needs to be rehearsed to the point of mastery via your preshot routine. The preshot routine needs to be overlearned because if you focus excessively on your components while you swing (aim, grip, stance, etc.), you create a conscious or coercive sense of movements versus a flow that is reactive and free.

Ashley, like many other top players, is to be congratulated for committing every day to getting beyond her doubt. If she has a clear picture of how she will execute her plan and manage her doubt, she and many others who suffer from this same mistake will find themselves in the winner's circle.

THE MENTAL MISTAKE #4

Perhaps the hardest mental lesson to learn in golf is to believe in your talent and be happy with your own game. This is especially true when you are playing with more experienced players or seasoned veterans. Comparison is constant, and many times you feel that you do not measure up to the reputations or playing abilities of others. You may even wonder if the other players are talking about you or feel that you do not belong in their playing group. Our final segment, from teaching and playing professional Dave Jones, has a strong mental testimonial that everyone can relate to. Dave addresses his not being as experienced as some of the players that he faced and how this created a lack of trust in his own game. Dave discusses his mental error and the frustration he felt in learning how to let go of others and ultimately create a foundation of self-belief.

My greatest mental mistake or shortcoming would be thinking in my mind that I was good or that I was a talented player,
but not believing totally in the talent that I possessed. I mean,
I thought I had a pretty good game, but I truly didn't believe in
myself, or not the level of believing that you need to possess
that creates unwavering confidence and produces great results. Whenever I would be playing with other players of
greater experience levels or backgrounds with sparkling résumés and strong reputations, I wouldn't believe in my talent
as much. Perhaps I was always looking at their games and
feeling like "Wow, they have such good games and they play
so much more solidly than I do," and this sort of made me a
bit intimidated. I don't know if it affected my confidence level
or not, but I never tried to show that I was intimidated on the
outside, but on the inside, I was a bit affected. I don't know if
I was consciously comparing myself to them, but I know that
I would become attached to their shotmaking and play and
that might have affected my psyche a bit.

Perhaps the main reason I felt like this when I was playing golf professionally was that I just didn't have the back-
ground or playing experience that most of the other guys on
the tours did. I mean, when I was growing up, I was more
interested in becoming a professional baseball player and I
really didn't play any junior golf at all. The only reason I
started playing golf really was to be with my dad. The players that are on the tours today are heads and shoulders
ahead of me when I was a junior playing baseball and moving into golf. If you look at the junior golfers of today, they
are veterans of hundreds of tournaments by the time they

(continued)

get to college, and the experience level that they have created for themselves by playing in lots of tournaments is enormous. What I had to do was just jump into the fire and get acclimated to learning by doing, and that meant playing golf and gaining experience by playing with stronger and more experienced players. It was a growing and learning experience for sure.

So, I feel that as I learned to believe more in myself and just play my game, the results and my comfort level in playing with other name players and in big tournaments tended to ease a bit, and I ended up playing pretty well and winning my first professional event by staying true to myself and my game and just doing my own thing. It sounds easy to simply say to "believe in yourself and just go play golf," but when it comes down to it, it may be the toughest aspect of playing tournament golf.

DR. BOB'S Rx FOR SUCCESS

The mental issues that Dave Jones talks about are typical of those of the millions of golfers who tee it up every day with other players in all types of recreational and competitive play. His viewing of himself as a good player but not fully believing in his talent is typical of many players who wear a mask of good swing mechanics and think they have a solid golf game. But these impostors crumble during performance rounds because their belief system is unstable. As Dave looked around at name players who had greater résumés or larger reputations than his, he devalued his talent and his positive self-image and confidence eroded.

While Cameron "stargazed" at the mass of talent around him on the PGA Tour, Dave did the same thing but on a smaller scale. This happens to players at every level of golf, whether junior, collegiate, or amateur. We look around and wonder about our ability and create doubt when what we need to do is to take care of our own business. By doing that, we take a big step toward attaining personal control. Letting go of others and taking care of number one (which is you) is the ultimate playing plan. It puts you in control of what you can do and places the onus of responsibility and "having to play well" on the other players. In essence, you are creating a zone of confidence and control and letting the other players fight it out among themselves.

Over time, Dave became more comfortable with the competition and other players and, inevitably, with himself and his talent. When he finally learned that only he can control himself and started to let go of the other players and their games and reputations, his own stock started to rise. Here are a few things that you can do to ultimately get you to a higher level of golfing efficiency and to create a foundation for believing in your talent.

FOUR IDEAS TO HELP GROW YOUR BELIEF SYSTEM

1. Remember, *you* are your golf game. That is, no one can play your game or think like you when you are on the golf course. You need to accept that on the golf course,

in a scoring situation, you are only able to hit the ball a certain way, a certain distance, and a certain trajectory. It is your way. Do not allow yourself to be swayed into thinking that you need to be doing things differently from what you normally do just because someone else does it another way. There is a time to accept that this is how you play, and there is a time to make appropriate changes. Here are a couple of specific strategies for you when on the course:

a. **Play your game.** Stay with your game plan and hit the shots you know you can hit. Do not hit a club that is not right for you. Hit the one that gets the job done! Do not allow yourself to be swayed by what other golfers are hitting.

b. **Be decisive about the type of shot you want to hit.** If you know that you want to hit a high draw, do not change your mind when you are over the ball. Stay committed to the shot and the plan.

By hitting the types of shots that you know you can hit or will provide a high percentage of success, you will build confidence and eliminate worry about poor results. It is vital that you take the time to develop these strategies on the range before you go play. As they say, practice makes relatively permanent. Therefore, practice the way that you want to play and the results will take care of themselves when you are on the golf course.

2. In everything you do in your golf . . . *you need to let go of others.* As you enter the golf gates, you need to tell yourself, *Today is all about me . . . I will let go of what others are*

doing or what they might be thinking. Give yourself permission to focus more on yourself than what is going on around you. You need to focus on yourself and your golf game. You cannot control others any more than they can control you. The sooner you let go worrying about what others may (or may not) be saying or thinking about you is when you have more energy to invest in your game.

3. *Make positive decisions about your game and shot strategy before you step onto the course and into your shot.* Being decisive about how you want to play and about what type of shot you want to hit eliminates much of the internal clutter and self-made noise that emanates from doubt. Remember that worry is a feeling of losing personal control and feeling vulnerable. The key word here is *feeling.* Feelings do not have to reflect reality. If you can focus on executing the proper procedure and dismiss the negative feelings that accompany the shot, you can move through the doubt and hit your shot with surprising accuracy and consistency. Having a game plan and specific shot strategy and sticking to it will replace the feelings of doubt and uncertainty with a sense of purpose and directedness.

4. *Learn to become comfortable with the uncomfortable. When you are in a tough situation, tell yourself right then, "This is a challenging situation . . . but I can handle it."* Composure is vital to playing great golf and is a key element to obtaining mastery and building confidence. However, to build a feeling of emotional comfort, you need to expose yourself

to difficult or new situations and learn to become comfortable with the uncomfortable. By introducing an unfamiliar element (such as playing with strangers, putting everything out—i.e., not taking gimmes—or playing with stronger or more experienced players) you will become more comfortable by virtue of the repeated exposure. Remember, anytime we do something the first time, it always seems difficult because it is novel. You don't know what will happen until you have been in that situation and experienced it firsthand! But the more times we do something, we learn from the experiences and adjust. I firmly agree with what former First Lady Eleanor Roosevelt said: "We must do the thing we fear. . . . The more times that we do it, the less its deathly grasp will have a hold on us." Doing the uncomfortable or facing unfamiliar situations can eventually lead us to a feeling of competence and comfort where we once experienced uncertainty and doubt. This is not only a vital golf lesson, but one we can take for every other area of our lives.

TAKE IT TO THE COURSE!

1. Make today . . . *your day!* Your day on the course is about you and only you. Forget about everyone else and what people are doing! This is your time. Use it. Choose to believe more in your talent than others'.
2. Hit the shot you know you can hit . . . functional is often more successful than fancy.

(continued)

3. On each shot you face . . . remember that this is a new moment and that this is the one that gets you going in a positive direction! This is how you create momentum.
4. After every shot . . . good or bad . . . either find something good to focus on or simply move on to your next shot.

TWO

I Hit the Ball When I Know
I Am Not Ready

*Every great mistake has a halfway moment, a split
second when it can be recalled and perhaps remedied.*
—Pearl Buck

THE BALL JUST SITS THERE!

A classic confrontation about physical activity and performance
execution occurred between two of the most famous ambassa-
dors of their respective sports: baseball great Ted Williams and
golfing legend Sam Snead. Their interchange is a perfect lead-in
to this chapter's premise.

Ted and Sam were together shooting a commercial and a
magazine ad for a large retail chain that they both represented
when the discussion turned to what was the most difficult activity in sport. The great slugger Ted Williams, known for his
bold swagger as well as his bat, maintained that hitting a baseball was the hardest motor activity in sport, bar none. He said
that stepping into the batter's box and facing a pitcher who was
only sixty feet away and throwing a round missile that could

knock you out was far and away the most difficult task in sport. Ted proclaimed that you had to decide in microseconds not only where the ball, constantly swerving in space was coming from, but where it was going and how to move the bat to meet the ball squarely. A tall order indeed! Ted pointed out to Sam that the pitcher always maintained a slight advantage because only he and perhaps the catcher knew beforehand what type of pitch would be thrown and where it was going. All this, plus the fact the ball might be moving at over ninety miles per hour, made Ted's statement extremely convincing.

Having heard Ted's enthusiastic and somewhat blunt dissertation on the complexities of hitting a moving baseball, Sam calmly replied to Ted that hitting a golf ball with a golf club moving at speeds of over a hundred miles per hour and directing that pellet to a desired location consistently was a much greater chore for the athlete. Hearing this, Ted Williams reportedly was aghast and bellowed, "You've got to be kidding me. . . . Hell, the damn ball just sits there waiting for you to hit it! It doesn't move! Not only that, you get to put your hands on it and put it on a tee! How in the world can you say something like that when the ball doesn't move compared to hitting a moving baseball?"

Sam looked back at his friend and replied in his famous Southern accent, "Yes, Ted, I can see your point, but in golf, we have to play our foul balls."

IN GOLF, WE HAVE TO PLAY OUR FOUL BALLS

We may never know what Ted said in response, but Sam's words hit home to every golfer who has ever played golf and baseball or any other sporting activity that involves a ball and a target. The difficulty in golf is to be able to step into each shot realizing that this shot will count in the final tally. In contrast, in a sport such as baseball, foul balls and missed swings aren't as penalizing as a missed putt in golf or a shot that goes out of bounds or into a water hazard. In golf, not only is the stroke counted, but add the penalty shots and you have put a big plus into your final tally. In baseball, it is often considered excellent if you can average one hit in every times three times at bat, and those fortunate enough to do this often find themselves inducted into the baseball Hall of Fame!

I realize that hitting a baseball is extremely difficult, but in golf we *do* have to play our foul balls, and there are no second or third pitches or bases on balls. Where you hit your ball is where you find it and then hit it again until you successfully sink the putt. You simply cannot bluff or wish your way to a good golf shot or score. You must perform well and execute quality golf shots and do that for the entire round. There are no letups or soft innings or even pitching errors. The result of each shot is up to you, and the final consequence is totally up to you, the performer.

Perhaps this is the reason for the trepidation and the doubt. Maybe we place such a huge psychological strain on the finished product that we distort our automatic motor movement and end up vacillating over the ball. Why is it that we have such a tough time stepping into the ball and behaving in a confident manner when the ball just sits there waiting for impact? And why is it that we step into the ball and worry so much when many of our recent shots have yielded positive results?

"TO ACT OR REACT?"— THAT IS THE QUESTION

Tiger Woods once stated that you should never make a mental mistake in golf because the ball is just sitting there waiting for you to hit it. Coming from perhaps the greatest player of all time, this comment makes complete sense. It is logical and philosophically sound, but as in all things in golf, it is much easier to discuss the issues rather than to create a working reality. Even though Tiger said it, I am sure that even the Great One has made his share of mental mistakes (although he must be onto something because he rarely unravels from a mental miscue). His reasoning comes from the basic fact that the ball is static (without movement) and so is the target. This means that the ball will not move until the golfer generates a force with the golf club to propel it from its original position. Therefore, it's imperative for a player to have everything that he wants to do to execute the shot planned before he steps to the ball to hit it. The only things that are moving are you and your golf club, and all of that activity is under your total control.

So why do golfers who are over a ball and know they are not ready to hit go ahead and swing anyway? Why would you swing when you are not sure of your shot plan? Because the root problem is so straightforward, this mental malfunction is one of the greatest mistakes that a golfer can make. Why don't we simply back away and start over? What exactly compels us to get it over with and hope for the best?

Many of us who play golf for recreational and competitive enjoyment didn't start out playing golf as our feature sport. Most of us grew up playing team sports and interactive games with great dynamic movement and physical flow. Sports such as soccer, baseball, basketball, hockey, and football were the norm for many of us. Perhaps the answer may lie in investigating the nature of these games.

SPORTS OF REACTION VERSUS PROACTION

First of all, each of these sports has a proactive and a reactive quality. For instance, a pitcher initiates movement by throwing the ball to the catcher. That is a proactive and dynamic movement. A proactive movement means one that emanates or springs forth from the athlete. The movement is self-initiated by the performer without the interaction of others or incoming objects. A pitcher initiates the primary action by deciding what type of pitch to throw, then proceeds into his windup and delivery. His movement is dependent totally on him and not on others or things moving around him in his environment.

Conversely, a reactive sequence takes place in orchestration with the pitcher's proactive movement. The batter must react to the moving pitch and swing the bat to meet the ball squarely to get a hit and get on base to score runs. In the flow in baseball, once you are on base, your task is to monitor the movement of the game and to run and steal bases so that you can score runs.

What I am discussing here is the reactive energy flow that has been prominent in most of our sporting lives. In each sport that I have listed above, a sphere or object is moving to or away from a target that is either stationary or has a defender who is moving as well to prevent you from scoring. The nature of these games is to monitor the movement and to anticipate the dynamics of motion and to move accordingly. Sports such as baseball, football, and soccer are reactionary and are dependent on a flow of motion that is constant and, unlike golf, on the participants' anticipatory skills to the ball, the target, and their surroundings.

Unlike golf, reactionary sports happen so quickly that they do not allow the mind to wander aimlessly toward negative thoughts or wayward senses of purpose. Reactionary sports depend on an immediate response to a stimulus, and because of the instant impetus acts must be instinctive rather than deliberate and well thought out, as is the case for every golf shot. Simply, in sports such as tennis, football, and soccer, the movement is so fast, you don't have time to think. You must move, react, and move some more.

In the self-paced sport of golf, the action is largely proactive rather than reactive. In golf you have more time to think . . . perhaps *too much time,* and that is where we get messed up! We spend too much time thinking about what we want to do with the shot instead of stepping in and swinging in a decisive manner. Overthinking usually ends up with tragic results. The key is to understand the dynamic interaction between the proactive and the reactive in hitting a golf shot.

PROACTIVE VERSUS REACTIVE GOLF

In playing golf and executing one shot at a time, the forethought or the cognitive creation of the shot is most important and allows the flow of the physical-movement sequence to happen. Simply, in golf, there is time to prepare and get ready. This could be considered the proactive segment of the golf shot. The preparation and pre-swing phase starts before the first step is taken to address the ball. After the planning and decision making is done and the golfer is sure of his shot plan, stepping into the ball and setting up and swinging are reactionary and responsive to the intended target. The great pro golfers of every era have known this, and when they are clear about what they want to do, they step in and simply react to the target in a reflexive fashion . . . *but the proactive part of the shot started long before they stepped in to address the ball.* You can even say that the physical routine is a reactionary result of all of the conscious deliberation that preceded the initial set over the ball.

This is what the best professionals in the world have learned, and this is how they get out of their own way from overthinking and overcontrolling. They understand that the key to successful golf shots is to become clear in the proactive phase so that they can swing freely during the reactive phase.

IF YOU'RE GONNA MISS, MISS 'EM QUICK!

In golf, one of the innate challenges is to take the time to think things through and to create a thoughtful strategy for the shot at hand. Once you have a well-thought-out plan, you can then initiate your well-ordered routine and perform the movements with purpose, fluidity, and confidence. One of the biggest differences between reactionary sports and a proactive sport such as golf is that we may have too much time on our hands to contemplate all of the things that can go wrong. Many times in golf we sabotage our talent by having too much clutter in our minds as we are walking from shot to shot. Upon stepping into the ball, we let our minds run adrift with doubt, worry, and the contemplation of what could happen, and then we end up swinging quickly just to get it over with!

This last sentence reminds me of a famous Lee Trevino quip: "If you're gonna miss 'em, miss 'em quick!" Many players end up doing just this . . . they rush their swings to move through the anxiety and finish the shot and move on until the next hurried moment. If you think about your own game and why you swing before you are ready, the reasons can be numerous, such as:

Common Reasons for Hitting Without Being Ready

1. I rush myself . . . I just don't take the time to get set.

2. I feel intimidated by my playing partners.

3. I feel nervous in front of strangers and just want to get the shot over with.

4. I feel that if I back off and restart my routine, my friends will say I am trying to be a "tour pro" and I will be chastised for slow play.

5. I am disgusted and I just want to finish the shot and the round.

6. I just wasn't thinking, I get careless.

7. Lack of focus and lack of recognizing when I am not really there for the shot.

8. I was just going through the motions—I was drifting.

9. I fail to recognize when I am rushing and I force the shot.

10. I hate to back off because I feel that it will cause me to hit a poor shot.

11. I feel that I can get away with the shot and it will work out okay without backing off.

12. I am impatient and just want to get things going.

These are just a few of the many reasons that golfers have given me through the years for why they go ahead and hit a shot without being fully committed and ready. But it isn't just an amateur error; numerous top professionals and world-class amateurs make the same mistake. Let's investigate a few of their stories and see if they can shed light on how to get more focused and ready to play great golf.

I HIT THE BALL WHEN I KNOW I AM NOT READY

THE MENTAL MISTAKE #1

Bob Lohr is a former winner on the PGA Tour and is now a certified master instructor for the Leadbetter Golf Academies. In discussing his mental mistakes, Bob addressed a number of issues that I have listed, but he was most fearful of what backing off might mean to other people or that he might interfere with his timing. A variety of things emanated from his interview that can help us understand why we hit without being fully committed and ready.

Regarding my golf, I think that managing the course was without a doubt my strongest asset as a player. What I lacked physically I gained by playing the golf course to my greatest strengths.

However, some of my biggest mistakes arose from hitting shots while second-guessing my plan while I was over the ball getting ready to hit it. This would lead me to doubt and I would fail to back off and start the process over again. I can't tell you how many times I was over a putt and I could feel something was wrong.

Now this could have been on the putting green or on the course and I would have this feeling that my aim and alignment was off, but I went ahead and hit the shot anyway, convincing myself that the end result would be okay. So, I would just go ahead and hit it or putt it and too often this breakdown in mental execution led to an unfavorable result. I wasn't able to really get control of this recurring mental mistake until I became confident enough and mature enough to finally step off and away from the ball and start my process over.

Many times I would be worried that if I did step off and start over, my playing partners would think poorly of me or I would be having timing issues (taking too much time for a particular shot) and so I would just go ahead and hit it.

I finally decided later in my career that I wasn't going to worry about other players or what they thought about my taking my time and I was going to make the commitment to myself from that point on that I would not play a single shot that would become sabotaged by doubt, hurrying, or poor planning.

DR. BOB'S Rx FOR SUCCESS

Bob Lohr's honesty in describing his inability to back off when he wasn't ready or feeling comfortable is a tribute to his recognition of the importance of getting your mind in the right place before you swing. The saying "hindsight is twenty-twenty" is clearly evident in his responses. I am sure that every golfer I interviewed for this book can look back and say to himself or herself, "If I had known then what I do now, things might have been very different." This means that a great many players had to find out via trial and error *what to do and what not to do* to create their personal path to success. This was certainly true with Bob Lohr. (Hopefully this book will help you avoid unnecessary years of failing via trial and error.)

Bob talks about feeling good about himself and of his ability to manage his ball around the golf course even though he felt he did not have the physical strengths of some of the other tour players. He talks of not being comfortable, of knowing intuitively that something was wrong even when he was warming up on the practice green before he headed to the first tee. But on the way to play he would try to convince himself that everything would turn out okay and he would go ahead and hit his shots anyway, which got him into trouble. He also discusses not backing off and starting over when he had doubt. He would try to fight through it and swing anyway, hoping that everything would work out all right. This is a subtle yet deceiving aspect of golf.

So many times we believe we can get away with the shot and hit it, and perhaps a few times during our round we end up with a good result. However, this is a poor strategy because when it comes down to a crucial shot and we swing when we are not ready, the result is oftentimes disastrous. Bob also talks about his feeling of being misaimed or misaligned, which created doubt and confusion and he would take this worry with him to the golf course. What we can infer is that this self-doubt and second-guessing made him tentative and diffident in his decisions and shotmaking. Bob also discusses how he would not back off because he was afraid of what other players would think of him, or that it would cause him to have timing issues in his golf swing. Also, a subconscious thought may have been that he would be fined for taking too much time and perhaps receive slow-play warnings from rules officials.

Bob Lohr teaches us that you should never hit a shot until you are fully committed and ready to swing to your target . . . ever. Bob clearly emphasizes this axiom in his last sentence. Bob made a commitment to himself that he would never allow others that he was playing with or officials to hurry him into hitting a shot without his being fully prepared to swing. This simple playing philosophy of not hitting a shot until fully ready is perhaps one of the greatest lessons that every player needs to learn and relearn, no matter his or her age or talent level.

THE MENTAL MISTAKE #2

Wayne Grady has been a PGA and Champions Tour member and also won the 1990 PGA Championship. In discussing his mental mistake, Wayne alluded to a number of points that everyone seems to suffer from, and many of these thoughts seem so utterly simple and sometimes random, but that is how the mind works. Wayne discusses his frustrations with just not doing what he knows he needs to do to get better.

The greatest mental mistake I make is that when I step into the ball and start to address it, a stupid thought might enter my mind. I mean like not a bad thought, but a stupid thought, such as I have just hit five balls perfect and I say to myself, "Don't screw this one up."

I know that I am thinking this dumb little thought and I go ahead and hit the ball anyway. I wonder, "Now why in the world did I think that? Where did that thought come from?" And for me to know better, well, that's when this game is so perplexing because everyone I know has done it. It's just that the best players don't do it very often.

But that is it for me . . . being over a shot and having a dumb, or perhaps the word is *stupid,* thought jump in my brain and I don't back off and start over.

It even happens when I practice sometimes. I am talking like when I hit four or five balls flush, I just swoosh one to the right and I say to myself, "Where in the hell is your focus?!" It's just a matter of getting your mind in the right spot and then just staying in the moment. But it is easier said than done.

DR. BOB'S Rx FOR SUCCESS

We can learn from Wayne Grady that everyone who plays this game is human, and that everyone . . . and I mean *everyone* . . . will suffer from these random thoughts of self-doubt and worry from time to time. What is so vexing for many of us is that they pop up when we least expect them, as is the case for Wayne.

The simplest way to deal with these thoughts is to acknowledge that you may have them and to let them pass. Do not make the mental mistake of trying to fight them head-on and saying to yourself, "No, I am not going to think about this thought . . . no, no, no!" This type of strategy only reinforces what you *don't* want to happen, and you end up only strengthening these negative and cluttering thoughts.

A better way to deal with these unwanted thoughts is to simply create a strong philosophy of saying to yourself, "It's no big deal . . . I am going to let it pass . . . it is just a stupid little thought." We find in the psychological literature that when you try to fight off a thought or suppress a thought, the thought gains in strength and arises even more.

So, I would tell Wayne to do a couple of things to get through this mental mistake. First, I would simply remind him that these thoughts are many times our own little voices of self-doubt. When you say to yourself, "Don't miss this one," you have to ask yourself, "Where did that stupid thought come from?" The answer would be *you*. So, the treatment for this mistake is to recognize that the voice is not coming from someone else but from you, and to smile and back off and tell yourself that is not what you want to think or even say to yourself. Second, as you are stepping into the shot or you are over the ball, instead of fighting the thought, simply allow this stupid or crazy thought to sift through your working consciousness and dismiss it and get your eyes and body focused back onto your precise target. The more we attempt to block something from our minds, the more it wants to creep in and take hold. A philosophy of passivity and dismissal tends to work best in this case. But if you hold that stupid thought and try to fight it while you swing . . . you have committed a serious mental mistake.

THE MENTAL MISTAKE #3

D. A. Points is fast becoming an up-and-comer on the PGA Tour and has been a rising star for the past several years after having a stellar amateur career and having a solid Nationwide Tour career and having now won on the PGA Tour. Points discusses his mental mistake of not being sure about his process when he is putting, but then going ahead and stroking the putt anyway.

> The toughest thing for me is when I am not putting well and not taking advantage of my opportunities that I am giving myself. I don't know exactly what it is, but I tend to start pressing or getting a bit discouraged and trying harder when I miss a few putts.
>
> But the thing that really gets me is when I am over a putt and I know what the process or task should be and I start to lose my focus and I go ahead and hit it, and I know that I wasn't really clear or sure of what I was doing, but I went ahead and putted it anyway.
>
> It's a bit difficult to say exactly what it is, but when things are going your way, it seems that the ball rolls on line a bit better and you don't worry about so many different things.

DR. BOB'S Rx FOR SUCCESS

D. A. Points's mental mistake is losing focus and having doubt in his putting but going ahead and putting anyway. Almost all of us at one time or another make this mental mistake, and some of us more frequently than we would like. Points speaks about not being sure of his line or his read, and it creates doubt as to what he truly intends to do. Filled with uncertainty, Points goes ahead and putts the ball anyway, knowing all along that he is not ready.

In golf, the error of confusion and lack of purpose shows up more often on the putting green than anywhere else on the golf course. Being uncertain about an upcoming putt hardly ever helps either putting confidence or stroke execution. This is because the closer you get to the hole, the more specific and precise your execution has to be. On the putting green, the ball can only do one of two things: it can either go in or it stays out. On the course and off the putting surface, you can get away with a missed drive or a wayward approach shot because you always have the opportunity of recovery. But on the putting green a putt that is missed is missed forever. There is no recovery or makeup for a missed attempt or sloppy execution.

D.A. talks of his thought process and his lack of clarity as to what exactly he intends to do. This uncertainty affects his confidence. We can learn from D.A. to make sure about our line and how we want to stroke the ball before we address the ball. D.A. also alludes to pressing and trying too hard. But judging whether we hit a good putt or not depending on the outcome is not a good way to judge putting prowess.

I would suggest to D.A. and to everyone else who suffers from this dilemma to do three specific things:

1. Before stepping in and addressing the ball, you need to establish exactly where you want the ball to roll and how hard you need to hit it. Having a clear picture and internal "feel" about how you will hit the putt is vital to putting success.

2. Stepping into the ball, maintain your "feel" awareness and commit to your putting line and execute the stroke and hit the ball as solidly as possible. If you can stay true to your putting plan and execute the stroke with a solid strike, you will find more balls finding the bottom of the cup. The key point here is to commit to your putting line and to *hit the putt solid*. The best putters in the world are always talking about the squareness of the putting contact when they are putting their best. You should strive to attain this same feeling as well!

3. After the ball has finished rolling (or has gone into the hole), reflect on your putt and establish whether you committed to your initial plan. Stay committed to making solid putts rather than judging a putt by whether it goes in or not. If you stay committed to the putting process, the process will work for you!

TAKE IT TO THE COURSE!

1. You never . . . ever . . . hit a shot until you are totally sure that your mind is clear and that your ball is going to your intended target. This is vital to your success!
2. If you are feeling a bit of doubt and worry about a shot . . . back away and recommit to your shot plan. This is also vital.
3. Remember, it is better to take a few more seconds to get yourself properly set than to spend five to ten min-

(continued)

utes in the woods looking for your ball that was hit from haste ... don't you think?

4. Be decisive. Knowing what you want to do before you step into the ball and address it is the best way to create a feeling of confidence. Decisiveness = confidence!

5. Understand that you may have a number of thoughts going through your head ... good, bad, and sometimes crazy thoughts ... this is natural. Simply allow bad thoughts to pass and get your eyes back into your target and swing with full intention and trust.

THREE

I Get Ahead of Myself—I Fail to Stay in the Moment

If you're not making mistakes, then you're not doing anything. I'm positive that a doer makes mistakes.
—JOHN WOODEN

FOCUSED IN THE MOMENT— HOGAN AND FLOYD STYLE

One of the most common sound bites that players who win tournaments make is how they stayed in the present moment and played one shot at a time. The statements "one shot at a time" and "stay in the present" have been uttered so often, it has become almost a cliché to tell a golfer to do this rather than saying "good luck." But we should not think that this is unusual or newsworthy, because for every great performer in golf, being absolutely engaged with the target and not allowing the mind to wander or get ahead of oneself has been the axiom for several decades.

Reportedly, Ben Hogan was on many occasions followed by his wife, Valerie, and he would pass her several times in the gallery and not even recognize her because his focus was so intense and entirely in the moment. Ben created a cocoon of concentration and did not allow his concentration to wander to external distractions such as family and friends. Ben was the ultimate poster boy of focus due to his uncanny ability to filter out the extraneous and fixate on his task, which was to hit the golf ball to his intended target.

Because of this immersion into his own performing world, Ben was given the moniker of the Wee Ice Mon by the Scots during the British Open in 1953. He exhibited a zonelike focus with a steely exterior and an icy demeanor that was not entirely fan-friendly. But to his credit, Ben was much more interested in hitting great golf shots and being totally into "his" moment than being appreciated by the golfing public. Ben's record and Major Championships victories are testimonials to his power of concentration and ability to stay engaged in the present moment!

Another golfer with a steely focus was Raymond Floyd. Raymond was known for his intense stare and the power to stay in his own world as he was hunting down the flagstick during the final holes of a Major Championship. It was often heard around the locker room that when Raymond had the lead or was close to securing a tournament win, he would almost "will the ball into the hole with his eyes," and that no one was better with a lead or closing the deal on a championship than Raymond due to his power to stay in the present moment and to play his own game. A testimonial to this was Raymond's own admission when he spoke of what it takes to win tournaments: "When I play my best, I can win anywhere in the world and against anybody." Raymond's ability to play his game, stay in his own little world, and focus in the here and now helped him win multiple Major Championships and enter the World Golf

Hall of Fame. For certain, Ben and Raymond had a lot in common, and that was to honor the moment!

"ONE AT A TIME"—NOTHING NEW . . . YET VITAL

As we discussed in chapter 2, people hit the ball when they are not ready for numerous reasons, and golfers likewise fail to stay in the moment and get ahead of themselves for numerous reasons. Think about it: How many times during the day do you drift and fail to stay on task? How many times has your wife, husband, or friend had to jostle you to get your attention back to the present moment because mentally you were someplace else? If this has happened to you, then you are guilty of not staying in the present moment.

If you are on the golf course during a shot and you are not totally focused on the activity, your mind tends to wander off in all sorts of directions. When this happens, your focus on the target is compromised, your attention to detail is scattered, and you start to hit balls astray left and right. Everything poor or deviant from what you wanted to happen . . . happens! This is because you did not pay attention to the shot at hand and you lost focus. As the great Bobby Jones said, the notion of playing one shot at a time is not new, but it is crucial to playing your absolute best.

This is why serious golfers (amateur and professionals alike) take the time through diligent training of their awareness skills to recognize when they become distracted. They recognize that distractions can be generated either internally or externally. Because the mind so easily seeks new information or reflects on things that have happened or could soon happen, it is important to realize the dimensions of internal and external distractions. Listed below are but a few of the distractions that can affect your ability to stay in the moment and play one shot at a time.

Internal Distractions (Things That Affect Our Sense of Control)

1. School, work, or personal relationships

2. Focusing too much on swing or technique

3. Thinking ahead about a difficult hole or match

4. Worrying about the score or negative results from the past

5. Thinking about winning or trying to impress others

External Distractions (Things That Affect Us Outside Our Control)

1. Environmental conditions such as wind, sun, or rain

2. Fans or crowds

3. Playing partners

4. Unexpected noises or events surrounding the play activity

5. Leaderboards or loudspeakers

When we are internally distracted, the voices inside our head misdirect our attention and lead us somewhere else.

Nongolfing thoughts of friends, parties to attend, or items to pick up at the grocery store on the way home are often the "warm culprits" of a misdirected mind. These thoughts come into our heads at the most inopportune times, such as when we are over the ball or actually swinging to the target. Golf-related internal distractions such as thoughts of score, results, and outcomes often interfere as well with our ability to focus on the shot at hand. As a result of this interference, we are quickly taken to a place where we did not want to go, which is the land of wasted shots and lost scoring opportunities!

Or, an airplane passing overhead or a dog barking could affect your concentration, or even a peek at a leaderboard—these are a few examples of external distractions. External distractions are items not within your personal control that affect your ability to stay in your bubble of concentration. Our inability to stay in touch with what we want to do in our moment of golfing execution limits our golfing potential.

THE MENTAL MISTAKE—I FAIL TO STAY IN THE MOMENT

A consoling thought about all of this, however, is that we are not alone in making mistakes of getting ahead of ourselves and not playing in the moment. Many of the world's greatest golfers that I have spoken to, such as Bob Charles, Charles Howell III, and Mike Hulbert, have all experienced the feeling of being out of sync and doing everything they can to regain control of the precious present moment. Here are a few of their testimonials, classic examples from prominent players who were willing to share their feelings about this major mental mistake.

My greatest mental mistake was not being able to close the deal and make some pars on the way in during the final day of the tournament. I remember having a six-shot lead with nine holes to play and I allowed my mind to wander and jump ahead. I just didn't do this once, but in several tournaments I let large leads slip away. I don't know, but my inability to stay in the moment and focus on what I needed to do caused me to not win as many tournaments as I would have liked.

I know that Peter Thomson and Bobby Locke had some of the strongest minds in golf because of their temperament and consistent demeanor. I think too many of today's players are too emotional and have too many large mood swings. Bobby Locke took on Sam Snead sixteen different times and defeated him fourteen of those sixteen. The thing about Bobby Locke was that when you watched him, whether he was in the lead or way behind, he never had a different pace in his step or his routine. He was always the same.

—Bob Charles, PGA winner and
Champions Tour professional

My greatest mental mistake is not staying in the moment. I tend to thinking too far ahead and get ahead of myself. I try and stay as much as I can on the task. My goal is to play a round of golf and divide it up into six three-hole segments. In each three-hole segment, my plan is to be at least one under for each set of three holes. But on each hole, my more immediate goal is to set my mind into each individual shot and

(continued)

make a mini-goal for that shot. In a sense, I am making tiny steps towards the finish line. However, I need to get better at this because I can only do this about eighty percent of the time. The other twenty percent I am probably getting ahead of myself.

—Charles Howell III, PGA Tour winner

My greatest mental mistake is to start thinking too much into the future, I mean thinking ahead. I just can't make the mistake of not staying in the present moment. I have to stay in the present. So, thinking ahead is my greatest mistake.

Maybe I am focused too much on how I stand to par in relation to my ongoing score in the round. Or I could be thinking about the eighteenth hole at Doral and the importance of the tee shot, but the problem with that thought is when I am only on the fifteenth hole of that day! So thinking ahead is definitely my biggest mental mistake.

—Mike Hulbert, PGA Tour winner and Champions Tour professional

The three golfers above all speak of common and consistent themes: projecting ahead and wanting to win, worrying about what others were doing or how they were going to explain themselves if they did not win. A few others spoke of being on one hole and jumping forward in their thinking to upcoming holes and sabotaging their efforts on the hole they were currently playing.

With so many touring professionals discussing their greatest mistake as failure to stay in the present moment, what should the remedy be? I will start and examine the testimonial of Hall of Fame member and multiple Major Championships winner Nick Price and provide some answers and insights.

THE MENTAL MISTAKE #1

The biggest mental issue for me is to stay in the moment. Staying in the moment means not getting ahead of myself. It is so easy to think, "I have four holes to play and two of them are birdie holes and I can get a couple of more birds in the bag." I think it is so easy to forget that you are supposed to focus on the task at hand versus thinking I need to make some more birdies.

Even when I was playing some of my greatest golf back in the nineties, that is the one thing I had to work on all the time and that was not getting ahead of myself. Even when I was in an unbelievable winning phase of my career, it was still hard not to get lost in the future, and it is something that I always have to work on. It is the one thing that you as a sport psychologist really must emphasize to your players, that they not forget what they are doing in the moment and to stay on the task of just playing this shot in the here and now.

I think that when you get really good at it, it is when your good days become really good and your bad days aren't as bad.

I mean, look at Tiger Woods; he is a really great example of someone who stays in the moment and doesn't allow bad

(continued)

shots or holes to upset his game plan or strategy. Even if he is having a bad day for Tiger, he is still around par because he is just fighting for every shot on every hole, all day long.

That is why he is so good . . . he just doesn't seem to drift . . . he doesn't get in front of himself. Tiger is one of those rare people that can let go of a bad shot and not get lost in trying to get a missed shot "back." He is so good at just moving on and getting into the next shot . . . that is really the key.

I think when I stay in the moment well, I am pretty good at it, or I have learned to be good at it. But, that is mainly because I have been focusing on it and working on it for a long time. It doesn't come easy, and even when you are doing it, you have to keep on doing it.

DR. BOB'S Rx FOR SUCCESS

Not only is Nick Price one of the greatest players to ever play the game, but he is spot-on when he discusses the key issues that take him from being in the moment. His comments about not being able to stay focused on the shot at hand are true for almost every golfer who plays the game. Almost everyone mirrors Nick's mistake of looking ahead, thinking more about one's total score instead of staying in the moment and executing to the best of one's ability the shot at hand.

Nick is like so many top players in that he gets a few under and starts to project in his mind on which of the upcoming holes he can pick up another birdie, rather than staying grounded and doing exactly what has gotten him into a scoring phase in the first place! What is fascinating is that even at the height of his

PGA career, he was always fighting this urge to project. After many years of working on staying in the moment, he can do a pretty good job of it, but it isn't easy and you always have to work at it.

Nick also notes that if you can become proficient at playing one shot at a time, your good days become very good and your bad days aren't all that bad! He discusses Tiger Woods as someone who does a great job of staying in the moment and, after a bad shot or hole, quickly dismissing it and moving on to the next shot. Nick notes Tiger doesn't get ahead of himself . . . he always stays in the moment and maximizes his energy in that moment. A great lesson for all of us to follow!

Amateurs make pretty much the same error in getting ahead of themselves, maybe not thinking of birdies but perhaps of pars or the likelihood of shooting a personal-best score or breaking 80, 90, or 100. When you become more focused on score and start to think ahead about results, rankings, or even winning, your thoughts are not in the here and now. Or, if you are always looking behind you and belittling yourself for making a few bogeys and squandering opportunities, you may then start to think ahead again in the hopes of getting some strokes "back."

The truth is that you will never get any shot back after you have hit it. That shot is done. That shot is history, and no amount of remorse, complaining, or cerebration will ever bring it back. You must move on. Back does not exist in golf. As I am always telling my students, "The result is . . . what it is . . . you must accept your result and move on!" That is the only way to think on the golf course . . . one at a time . . . all day long. Both Nick Price and Bobby Jones were outstanding golfers who realized the value of playing one shot at a time and found out that it takes a long time to truly learn it. But you do not have to spend years learning the way Nick and Bobby did; just remember to get your mind back into your task and you will save yourself an immense number of strokes and a lot of worry.

THE MENTAL MISTAKE #2

Suzann Pettersen is a bona fide star on the women's professional golf circuit. Not only is she one of the most physically fit lady golfers on the tour, but she is a wonderful athlete who plays all over the globe. Suzann, an attractive blonde from Norway, is known for her dynamic swing and fierce competitive nature. Because of her fiery personality and dogged determination, I believe that whatever business or professional field Suzann entered, she would probably excel. Suzann has played in multiple Solheim Cups and is a major champion.

Suzann revealed that her greatest mental mistake was not taking care of things in her control when she was in the middle of an intense competition. She admitted that she became a bit lost, and this caused her to deviate from her optimal performance state. Her story is the ultimate model for how one's greatest mistake can become one's most valuable lesson.

My greatest mental mistake may have been that I lost my focus on what I should have been doing and was focusing on things around me more than taking care of what was right in front of me. I also consider this mental mistake a blessing because it taught me what I needed to learn and how to overcome my weak areas or deficiencies.

(continued)

This happened at the 2007 Kraft Nabisco Championship, which is a major tournament on the LPGA Tour, and I bogeyed my last four holes to shoot a seventy-four and finish in a tie for second. Morgan Pressel was the winner, but I felt that what I learned from this poor finish has helped me to achieve an entirely different level of personal performance.

In particular, as I was coming down the finish, I was lucky enough to have had several people who videotaped the finish, and I was able to watch myself later and see that my preshot routine and behaviors were not the same at the end of the tournament as they had been previously in the week or during the last round.

On hole number sixteen specifically, when I was over the ball preparing to hit, I must have taken three or four extra seconds, and that was perhaps caused by my self-doubt about which club I should be hitting and questioning my decision. I was a bit out of sync and it showed up in my routine.

Through my own inspection of the videos and self-analysis, I figured out what had happened and I was able to correct it and turn it around and win the next major. So, you can really learn more from your mistakes and your failures and it really is the greatest learning curve that you can give yourself . . . that is, to put yourself in the middle of winning and to not achieve the victory, but also to adapt and to say, "What do I need to learn from this?"

This awareness helps you to create a maturity of memories that you can draw from and help you when you are in the middle of a tough or difficult situation and keep you in the present moment. But, the truth is that it all starts from the

(continued)

inside and not from the outside. When you can face the reality and say, "This is what I need to do and I have done it before," it makes the situation easier because you just stay in the moment and do what you have to do.

DR. BOB'S Rx FOR SUCCESS

That Suzann Pettersen can look at her mistake objectively and then turn it into a positive for future events is testimony to the power of evaluation and adaptation. Realizing she made a large mental error in not taking care of the events in front of her, she actually learned from that mental error in one major tournament to win the very next major. Now that's impressive! We can learn from Suzann's revelation that:

1. You always need to look at your performance, good or bad, and analyze what went well and what went wrong. One of the shortcomings that you make when you are playing well is that you hardly acknowledge what you are doing that allows you to stay in the moment! When golfers play well, they just assume that their golf is created by good swings. They forget or fail to realize that the way they assessed the situations and created shot plans gave them the pinpoint focus for accurate play. Most golfers tell me that when they are playing well, they aren't thinking about anything at all . . . they are just looking at the target and playing golf. The key element is that when you are playing your best golf, your focus is on the target

and not on yourself. When we start to play poorly, our focus becomes misdirected on either the trouble or our mechanics.

Suzann had the good fortune of reviewing videotapes of herself in competition, which allowed her to analyze her behavior and sense that her routine was out of sync. This lack of order in her routine was created by a lack of decisiveness in her shotmaking. Via the videotape, she could review her routine and become more aware of the nuances of her behaviors in her preshot procedure. She learned that heightened anxiety and stress (such as in a major tournament) tends to alter normal behavior and either speeds up or slows down one's routine. From that point on, she made certain to maintain her rhythm and sense of timing while performing her routine. This adherence to her preshot routine helped her to stay in an optimum state of directed flow. By practicing her routine and understanding exactly how much time she needed for each segment and training endlessly on these various maneuvers, her routine become automatic and better timed. This "overlearning" of her component behaviors allowed her to play with more efficiency, without spending too much or too little time over the ball, and led to her first LPGA Major Championship win!

2. By virtue of her recognition skills, Suzann could realize when she was becoming out of sync and when her arousal levels were heightened. Because she had experienced this situation before, she was better able to understand in the heat of competition how to handle nicely this difficult situation. *The required action cure here is to understand that any past failure does not have to mean*

doom and gloom in the present or in your future. You need to realize that you have been here before . . . you have prepared yourself for this moment . . . you now have the recognition skills to understand the event for what it truly is . . . and you can take the appropriate remedial steps to alter the distortion and to provide yourself a base of clearer thinking and smarter options for action.

3. What is most impressive about Suzann Pettersen's testimony is her talk of her "maturity of memories" and her knowledge that she now has the requisite skills to handle difficult situations with grace and effectiveness. Another vital element we can learn from her story is that you can only control you. Everyone else and the events around you are totally out of your personal control. Suzann made the common mistake of looking around and perhaps worrying about what other players were doing instead of focusing on her own game. This is perhaps one of the most common, yet very human, errors that we make as golfers. From Suzann's revelation, we learn one essential element: Your golf game is all about you! You need to quit worrying about other players and what they might be doing. Get into your own game and take control of the only person that you have any control over—you. The sooner you can get focused and control what you have in front of you, the sooner you start to play your best golf!

DR. BOB'S Rx FOR STAYING IN THE MOMENT

1. First of all, understand that this is a *new* moment . . . this is not the *past*. You do not have to replay the past nor does the past always have to be your present. Things can change as long as you do not drag your past into the present moment. Let go of your past and focus on the shot or event in front of you. This is the *first* step to being in the present moment.

2. Second, recognize the shot or event for what it is . . . not for what it means to you in personal recognition, money, or fame. For example, say you are coming down the stretch in an important event and you are on the final hole. You have just hit your drive to the center of the fairway, and you now have a 150-yard shot to an island green surrounded by water. Many times before you have hit into the water and botched your score because you had gotten ahead of yourself with your thinking and your desire to win so badly. You have suffered terrible anguish over this hole and feel that this hole has your number. Every time you come into this hole you feel snakebit. *It is absolutely crucial that you let go of the perception of what has happened in the past or what could be and get into WHAT IS!*

   Your approach shot of 150 yards is just that . . . a 150-yard shot . . . nothing less and nothing more. The physical requirements for this shot will still be a 150-yard strike to a target . . . no matter how much it means to you to win or to shoot the lowest score of your life!

The ball and the physical dimensions of the situation are unaffected by your thoughts or perception of the event. Your perceptions of grandeur are not the physical reality of the given situation. When we start to think about what a shot could mean to us perceptually and personally, the shot then takes on a different, if not higher, meaning. But the shot will remain just what it is . . . a 150-yard shot that deserves your full intention to be hit with purposefulness and positive intent.

So the *second* step you must take to be in the present moment is to realize that the shot you are currently facing has physical properties that do not change due to your perceptual state. Do not let your perceptions about the event alter your performance capability to hit the shot the physical situation demands.

3. The third step to not getting ahead of yourself and to staying in the present is to focus entirely on the particulars of the given situation. What are the exact demands for the present shot? You must assess the conditions of the shot before you can make a prudent and informed decision about it. You must assess the yardage, the lie, the distance to the pin or particular landing areas, and, most important, your assets for what you can accomplish at that moment. Once you have thought the shot through, you must make a clear and firm decision about what you are going to do with this shot now! This is the *third* step you must take to be in the present moment.

4. Once you have established what you want to do and how you are going to hit the shot, you must go through your preshot ritual of physical behaviors that match your

mental state of hitting the ball to your target. This means that when you step into the ball to address the shot, you must not delay or take extra waggles or looks to "feel" comfortable. Your routine is an established set of physical and mental behaviors that should run automatically. That is why a routine is a routine. Your automated routine becomes nonconscious—you should not have to consciously monitor or think about what you are doing. The behaviors simply flow one after another. This helps to explain how when you are playing your best golf, you aren't thinking about anything other than the ball's going to the target. You are simply getting into your routine and looking at where you want the ball to go and swinging to that visual image. When we experience anxiety or self-doubt, we tend to want to take control, and in essence we overcontrol and try to steer or help the ball, which hurts us with poor shot execution.

In Suzann's case, she may have performed several extra behaviors or mannerisms while addressing the ball that she thought would help her to feel more "comfortable and in control" but, in reality, were observable signs that trouble was brewing or doubt was manifesting within her. The *fourth* step to being in the moment is to adhere to your preshot routine and to allow your automated behaviors to flow as you have overlearned them through repetition.

5. The fifth step to staying in the present moment and not getting ahead of yourself is to engage yourself visually with your target and to stay committed to your intended shot plan and target. While getting ready to swing, your thought should be of the ball's going to the target. An-

other way to think of it is to take a last look at your target and to simply swing to your last-look memory. But the kicker to all of this is to engage your visual sense to a picture that you want to achieve . . . *not* to where you want to avoid. So many players generate a negative picture as they are about to swing, and inevitably your body gives you what you were last focusing upon. It doesn't do any good to focus on the flag on the green if your last look or last image in your head is of the ball splashing into the water. So, you must engage your visual system with the ball's going to where you want it to go! This is the accuracy dimension in visualization. Staying visually engaged in obtaining information for direction helps to keep you in the here and now rather than self-stimulating your visual memory and drudging up poor performances of the past. The *fifth* step is to engage your senses in the present moment to what you want to achieve now and exactly where you want your ball to go.

6. The final step to being in the present moment is to accept the shot that you have just hit. This means that if the result is good, bad, or just okay, you can interpret the result with a neutral focus and without negative or critical judgment. If you are frustrated that the move was incorrect, the time to make an adaptation should be right now. So many players berate themselves and take their negativity and personal garbage with them from shot to shot, which makes them vulnerable and overly aroused or too emotional. This out of control arousal clutters their thinking and judgment for the next shot. It is imperative to your golf game to take the

time to analyze and make a correction if the shot result was poor and to understand whether the mistake was mental or physical. Understanding what just occurred and making the correction and moving on is the way to put closure on a recent event. Obtaining closure and being able to accept your result is vital so that you can move on to the next shot with renewed focus and enthusiasm. The *sixth* and final step to being in the moment is to analyze and accept the result for what just occurred, and if necessary to make the appropriate correction for future play and to move on without negativity and self-sabotage.

TAKE IT TO THE COURSE!

1. Stay present. Focus on the shot at hand. The only time that you can do something about your golf game is *now*. Get into this shot and target!

2. If you find that your thoughts are focused on your score or results . . . tell yourself to *stop*! Back away from the ball and recommit yourself into the mental plan for this shot. Dismiss the numerical value or importance of the shot such as par, birdie, or bogey and get into the physical aspects of this shot!

3. Accept your result . . . no matter if the shot is good, bad, or just okay. You must accept. Failure to accept your result means that you are hanging on to the past.

(*continued*)

Let the last shot go and move into the next shot with renewed focus and vigor. Remember, a shot is just a shot. . . . It all counts as one.

4. Adhere to your preshot and preputt routine. The automation and fluidity of your routine will help to insure that your mind is in the right place and give you the best chance of hitting your best shot.

5. The only person that you should care about or control is . . . *you*. Forget about all others and what they are doing or shooting. Get into your own shot and game and immerse yourself into being the best you can be at this moment.

FOUR

I Do Not Commit to My Shot or Game Plan

A man who has committed a mistake and does not correct it is committing another mistake.
—CONFUCIUS

FOUR WORDS WITHOUT CLEAR MEANING

"Commit to the shot." These four words have been uttered by golfers, teachers, television commentators, and serious students of the game for the past several years and to the avail of almost everyone who plays, but few know what it means to commit to a shot. Oh, we have been lectured, admonished, and motivated to commit to the target or commit to a feeling, but what does it mean in playing a golf shot? Should I be visualizing my shot while standing behind the ball, or should I be using positive self-talk to psyche myself up into going for a treacherous pin? Even some of the mentally toughest players in the history of golf admit that their greatest mistake was the failure to commit. Hall of Fame member Raymond Floyd told me:

> I guess that my greatest mental mistake was that I lost my commitment when I stepped into and addressed the ball. I always try and have a strong commitment before I step into and address the ball, but somehow I lost that mental strength at times and wavered when I got over the ball.

Raymond speaks of having a strong mental conviction to his shot prior to stepping into the ball, but just prior to swinging the club, he lost his commitment. This seems peculiar . . . what was it that he lost and where did it go? What did he mean when he said that somehow he lost his mental strength? How could Raymond Floyd, one of the all-time greatest players and mentally toughest competitors that ever graced the links, lose his mental resolve? And if Raymond Floyd has encountered this dilemma, then I am sure that most of the golfing public suffers from this affliction as well.

As we will discuss in this chapter, commitment to your shot means a variety of things, and each is vitally important to the other. You will also learn that each of us holds a personal interpretation of what being committed means, and that our subjective view is paramount to our golf performance. Commitment has multiple interpretations that interact with one another to establish a foundation for optimal performance. But first, we need to explain what commitment is and also what it is not. We will also define the different subsets that commitment encompasses so that we can apply some meaning to a word that appears ambiguous.

DEFINING THE AMBIGUOUS (COMMITMENT)

Because we need to understand how players use the word *commitment,* I think it would help to define the word from a basic level. Used as a noun, it means "the act of committing or the state of being committed." It is also a "pledge or promise," such as "I have made a commitment to marry this person and be good to them for the rest of my life." Using the word in this way, couples during a marriage ceremony pledge their troth or loyalty to one another and promise that they will provide for each other in the future.

We also use *commitment* to stand for "the act of binding yourself (intellectually or emotionally) to a course of action." Being actively engaged or involved means that we commit ourselves to an activity at a specific time. The word can also mean "an engagement or involvement to something or someone." An example of this is when we commit to someone in a personal relationship or when we commit ourselves to a worthy cause or charity function.

Commitment can further be defined as a consignment, such as when one is consigned to prison or to a mental institution. "To commit someone" or "have them committed" means that an order is decreed by a psychiatrist that a person be placed in a mental institution for observation or for treatment. Taking these multiple meanings and wrapping them into a composite picture, it means that when we commit, we are creating a promise, pledge, or a proclaiming action that signifies that something will be done in the immediate future.

YOUR COMMITMENT—
YOUR GOLF GAME

Each of the preceding word examples can hold a key to why we use the words *commit* and *commitment* when we speak of playing golf and hitting golf shots.

First, when we commit to a shot, we are engaging in a moment of performance and a process that elicits a future behavior for when the ball will be struck. Second, when we are totally committed to a shot, we are pledging a degree of loyalty to ourselves, holding ourselves accountable for the action that we are about to execute. Third, by committing to a plan, we are committing to something tangible, such as swinging a club in a certain fashion that will move the ball a designated distance. The importance of commitment in golf comes back to being bound by a promise to yourself. It is about the relationship that consists of you, your ball, and your target.

For example, if we use the institution of marriage as a metaphor for golf, we find that the most successful marriages consist of a number of elements. According to family and marriage-counseling research, commitment is one of the most crucial ingredients for long-term marital success. It seems logical that a top priority would be a commitment to be loyal and steadfast to a spouse. But committing to your spouse is just one of several attributes that are required to have a lasting and successful marriage.

First on the list is that people are committed to marriage itself, then that they are committed to the other person. Love, communication, and compatibility are all on the list, but commitment was considered the top priority! That commitment has multiple aspects in marriage relates directly to the multiple aspects of commitment in your golf game.

YOUR GOLF GAME: YOUR MOST INTIMATE RELATIONSHIP

Just as in a marriage, golfers have a list of items that they need to commit to in shotmaking. These items include:

a. Commitment to your game or shot plan

b. Commitment to the club that you are using and the type of shot you will hit

c. Commitment to your overall shape of shot and trajectory

d. Commitment to your final target destination

e. Commitment to your swing key or swing cue

f. Commitment to your preshot routine

g. Commitment to the present moment

h. Commitment to being committed

i. Commitment to yourself and your talent

As I have presented them here, multiple stages of commitment are present in each golf shot. Your shot plan, your target, the club that you will be using, your preshot and preputt routines, and your commitment to yourself and the moment are all part of commitment. Since golf is the most intimate relationship that you have with yourself (in a dynamic setting and on the golf course), you have to be honest with yourself about honoring your commitment to a shot or plan. It is vital that you commit to the idea that you will persistently be committed. It is also crucial that when you are into a shot, you stay committed to your plan of action and that you do not allow yourself to simply go through the motions of your routine without being 100 percent engaged with your shot. Hall of Fame member Greg Norman addressed this aspect when he discussed his mental mistake:

I would say that my greatest mental mistake through the years has been to not commit one hundred percent to the shot. I mean, there are a number of different mental mistakes you can make as a player, but not committing to your plan is the main difference between playing well and playing poorly.

When you are playing well, your mind is clear and your shot plan is solid. When you are playing poorly or not as well as you would like or know that you can play, you tend to change your mind a bit too much and then that leads to indecision and lack of trust. When you commit to your shot or plan totally, the result usually takes care of itself.

We can learn from Greg's insight that when he made the choice of being 100 percent committed, it made a significant difference in the clarity and decisiveness that he could put into the shot. Greg points out that we can make a number of mental mistakes, but not taking care of your commitment in your shot plan is the major difference between success and failure.

Greg also mentions that when you are not committing or playing well, you tend to have more doubt and fail to trust yourself. Lack of trust leads to tentative play, and instead of having a definite shot plan to carry out, most of us try to avoid making a mistake, which leads to more self-doubt and poor swings. The doubt and lack of commitment was the initial failure that led us to poor results. Greg's statement suggests that when you take care of the essential little elements, the big picture turns out well.

THE MENTAL MISTAKE—I DO NOT COMMIT TO MY SHOT

Raymond Floyd and Greg Norman are not the only famous golfers who have revealed that their major mistake was not being committed to a shot. A host of other golfers that I have spoken with also mentioned failing to commit as their Achilles' heel. Many of these touring professionals list not being committed to the shot as a precursor of other mental issues, such as a lack of focus, lack of trust, and deviating from their normal routine during a pressure-filled moment. Kelly Froelich from Paris, France, is a young, rising star on the women's professional golf tours, and she admits not being able to commit to her swing of the club during a tournament round the way she does in a practice round:

My mental mistake that I make is that I just don't make the same swing on the course that I know I should make. It is a thing of confidence or trust. Perhaps my sense of commitment should be stronger, I am not sure, but I know that I am not truly committing to my shot the way I know that I should.

The way I practice now is helping me to be more committed, and with the things you and I are working on, I feel a stronger sense of confidence in my ability to do that. If I can commit to my shots and execute that plan, my game will be a lot better.

Kelly intuitively knows when she has not committed to her swing of the club. She talks about working on her commitment during practice and is confident that if she can train herself to commit to a specific plan during any one shot, that will help her swing confidence during her tournament rounds.

Another player who addresses the issue of sticking to basics and remaining committed to a few essential items is England's Justin Rose, PGA Tour winner and 2013 US Open champion.

My mental mistake is that I just don't adhere to my basic fundamentals. I mean, I have a simple game plan that is made up of some basic things that I have to do in order to allow myself to play my best.

When I go through this checklist and I make sure that I am doing the things that I know I need to do, then everything is

(continued)

going to work out okay. But, I seem to get into trouble and play below my level of talent when I don't do what I know I should be doing. It is sort of hard to explain, but I know when I am doing the right things, everything will take care of itself. The results—the good ones and good shots—seem to take care of themselves, but I have to do my thing consistently in order for everything to happen the way I want it to.

Justin speaks of having a list that he runs through that helps him to honor his commitment and has become a part of his overall process.

The essential item that we can learn from Justin Rose is that when he does not commit to his core principles, he does not play well. This is a major mistake of anyone who is competent in his or her field, whether it is golf, baseball, or business. Justin speaks of knowing when he is doing the right things and when he is not doing them. Getting to a "yes" mind-set that suggests you will do what you know you can do is known as compliance. The term *compliance* means that you will do what you say you are going to do. It is a basic element of getting to yes. A common statement that I hear from top athletes in a variety of sports who fail to achieve compliance is *"I know what it is I need to do, I am just not doing what I know!"* These athletes need to get back to adhering to their basics.

Another young golfer who admitted that he does not commit to his shot or game plan is Jonathan Moore. Jonathan is a former NCAA Division I champion and also was a member of the victorious US Walker Cup team in 2007. Jonathan came down the last hole in a match that would decide the fate of the

Walker Cup. On the final hole during the matches, Jonathan was on a long par 5 and had 248 yards to the green for his second shot. Jonathan adhered to his routine and hit a 4-iron to five feet and made the putt for eagle, clinching the US win. Jonathan, much like Justin, also claims that his failing to commit to his game plan and shot sequencing tends to hold him back.

> My greatest mental mistake is that I fail to trust my assessment and planning while I am stepping into the ball to hit the shot. I fail to trust myself and my planning and it directly affects my ability to execute properly. If I can commit myself to adhering to my shot plan and allow myself to do what it is that I know I need to do . . . everything else falls into place.
>
> I know that when I have done this in the past, I have had success in almost everything that I have played in, but I constantly need to remind myself that the planning and assessment is just as crucial, if not more so, than actually swinging the golf club itself.

Jonathan speaks of the necessary ingredient to constantly remind himself to do the things that work for him and to commit to them. Jonathan, much like Justin and Greg, experientially and intellectually understands that when he complies with his shot plan and commits to doing the things that he knows are effective, he will ultimately be successful. His last sentence is vital to understanding how committing to your plan is a part of the overall shot. Jonathan feels that his planning and assessment of the shot and committing to that plan is just as important as the physical striking of the ball. I couldn't agree more!

Another golfer who lists not committing to the shot as her main mental mistake is LPGA and European Tour player Maria Hjorth. Maria addresses the concepts of trust and commitment and suggests that both are keys to her playing her best:

> I think my biggest mistake for me and probably many others is that I fail to trust myself and commit to the shot. This is such a basic thing, but I really don't know which comes first, the trust or the commitment. I believe it is trust, because if you can trust, then the commitment is easier to do.
>
> The better that you become and start to have some success, the easier it becomes, but again, I think you have to really commit yourself to the idea that you know what you want to do before you step into the shot and trust that everything will turn out for the best. That is hard to do every time, but the more that you can do it, the easier it tends to become and especially when things are starting to go well for you.

Maria points out that if you can trust, then the ability to commit is easier. As you achieve some success, it becomes easier to trust and commit. This is similar to the chicken-or-the-egg question: Which comes first? I think most of us would agree that when you are playing good golf, it is fairly easy to trust your decisions and to honor your commitments.

However, it becomes hard to play well and trust if you lack the initial commitment to play the shots you know you can't hit! What I mean by this is that when you are unsure or feel negative about a shot, it is hard to force yourself to let go and simply trust. When we human beings feel insecure, threatened, or out of control, we tend to tighten our grip and manipulate whatever we are doing. This is contrary to the idea of trust. Trust is about allowing the swing to come forth rather than coercing or forcing the movement. Trust is about giving yourself permission to swing freely. Therefore, trust in the golf swing must first be acquired from a foundation of successful attempts and competence. Without physical competence in a specific movement or swing, little if any trust can ever be established.

Maria states that you have to really commit yourself to the idea that you know what you want to do before you step into the shot to hit the ball. Although Maria talks of the difficulty of doing that every time, the more times that you can truly commit to doing something, the more that you are able to trust that this procedure is effective, the easier the subsequent shots become. Maria goes on to say that when you are having success, things become easier, and this is when you can start to build positive golf momentum.

PGA and Champions Tour member Jim Thorpe discusses the perplexing (and quite common) issue of not honoring your commitment when you are over the ball and changing your mind and failing to back off:

The mental mistake I make is that I don't honor my commitment when I am over the ball. For some reason or another, I change my mind and I want to change my club. I can't seem to make a decision and stick with it. I need to do a better job of trusting my instinct and my first choice and then to stick to it. For example, I'm stepping in and addressing my ball, then a gust or even a puff of wind will sweep my ear or come into my

(continued)

> face, and I start to doubt and question whether I need to make a change.
>
> The real mistake is that sometimes I don't back away. I need to trust my decision that I first have when I am deciding my shot plan and go with it.

Jim brings to light the common situation when players are not sure what they want or they become distracted, but fail to honor their commitment to not hit the ball until they are 100 percent sure or ready. (This is linked to our Mental Mistake #2 in chapter 2, "I Hit the Ball When I Know I Am Not Ready," page 38.) The failure to commit creates doubt and confusion and translates into a swing that produces a poor result almost every time! Jim does a nice piece of self-evaluation when he proclaims that he needs to do a better job of trusting his instincts when he is over the ball and either go with his first decision or back off and regroup.

We learn from Jim that the simplest of things, such as a bug whistling in our ear or a sudden shift of the wind, tend to throw us out of our rhythm, and it is up to each of us to commit to our plan or step away. But the real lesson is that failure to commit only leads to mistrust and poor swings.

Our final disclosure about mistakes of commitment comes from University of Tennessee–Chattanooga golf coach, Mark Guhne. Coach Guhne is also a PGA teaching and playing professional and discusses at length what he sees in young players as a failure to commit not only to their shot plans, but to their overall preshot routines and their practice habits, and how a lack of commitment transfers into life as well.

As a coach, I see my kids not staying committed to their game plan or routine. I think the major thing that they have or need to learn is to really commit themselves to the shot at hand and let everything else go. Lack of commitment to a specific shot or strategy creates inconsistency, and that is where it always shows up.

I think the lack of commitment is transferable to everything in golf and in life. I see players that are so-so committed to practice, and they do the same thing in a tournament situation. So, the idea of practicing your commitment and honoring it every day in practice and in a tournament situation is something that is vital to becoming a really good player.

For me, it is something that I am trying to do in my own game as a playing professional . . . and I will tell you that it really works. When I have honored my commitment to a shot or game plan, my scores tend to take care of themselves.

But, for a large number of younger players, they really need to learn how to commit and what it really means to be and stay committed to the shot process.

Coach Guhne describes the number one mental mistake that he sees in his younger players as a failure to commit to their shot plan and also failing to commit to that process in practice as well. He discusses the need to learn how to commit to a single shot and to let the results of score, outcomes, and numbers go. His insight also suggests that younger players tend to become a bit too wrapped up in results and forget that the consistency of their play and of their commitment is what provides a good result at the end of the day.

DR. BOB'S Rx FOR SUCCESS:
YOU MUST COMMIT . . . OR QUIT!

Commitment is a multifaceted dimension that involves self-motivation and self-awareness for playing your best golf. Failing to commit to your shot or game plan is evidenced by the doubt and trepidation that you will encounter when you are over the ball. *The cure for this mental mistake is to understand that either you commit 100 percent to your shot before you step into and address your ball . . . or you don't commit at all!* Committing to your shot is as straightforward as knowing that the opposite of black is white. There is no gray area in the arena of commitment. *Either you commit or you might as well quit!* Why do I say this? Because if you have what Coach Mark Guhne suggested, a "so-so" commitment, your shots only have a so-so chance of turning out well. You will only be good part of the time. Your success will be random. Committing 100 percent is not a random process. You must do it each time for every shot you hit. This mind-set is created by structure and decisiveness. To be at your very best, here are some thoughts about how to commit to each shot with 100 percent effectiveness.

FIVE IDEAS TO CREATING A
COMMITTED MIND-SET

1. **Understand that committing to a shot begins *long* before the club is swung.**

   As you are stepping up to your ball and assessing the lie (or placing your tee into the ground), take the time to assess all of your options. Choose the shot that you *know* you can hit and the one that you *know* can be most effective at producing the desired result. Process the shot in your mind and visualize the successful execution of the shot with the intended shape, ball flight, trajectory, and even where the ball will end up. Having an absolute and crystal-clear picture of what you want to do with the shot breeds decisiveness and confidence that you have selected correctly. Having a clear plan fuels the ability to commit to hit a well-thought-out shot.

2. **Before you address the ball, produce the correct motion that you want to create with a rehearsal swing.**

From behind the ball and before you step into the address position, rehearse the actual motion of the shot you want to hit. Making one or two actual (real-time) swings prior to stepping into the address position helps to reinforce and preset your body's motor system and prepare it for the correct sequencing and body movement. Without a proper or real rehearsal swing, you are going into the shot cold and you are not creating "movement confidence" by confirming in your mind the feeling of how you want to swing the club. Having a strong body feeling of how you want to swing helps to reinforce movement confidence as you step in and address the ball.

3. **As you are stepping in and addressing the ball, visually commit to your target with your eyes and reconfirm to yourself what you are going to do and where you want the ball to go.**

One of the prime areas for players to back down or lose their sense of commitment is when they take their first steps to the ball to enter the address position. As you are stepping in and aiming the clubface to your target, adjust your stance and focus on your external target (as well as aim at your intermediate target). Directing your visual focus on where you want the ball to go will help you commit to the swing feeling that this is what you want to do and where you ultimately want the ball to travel. Having a clear target fresh in your visual memory helps to insure a committed swing to it.

4. **As you are ready to initiate your swing, take a final look at your target and reaffirm your commitment that everything is okay and that the ball is going to your target.**

   During the final few seconds when you are getting settled into making the initial backswing away from the ball, take a final look at your target and confirm that you are in a *go* state and that everything is going to work out well. This is the trusting phase, and if you have committed to each step prior to this point, the swing should be performed automatically and flow with authority and confidence. If you have doubt or any trepidation as you are taking your final look at the target, you need to be aware that you are not committed and to back away and recommit to the shot and start over. Having a strong sense that you have done all that you can do will allow your swing to run off automatically.

5. **Accept your result and know that because of your commitment you have given the shot your best effort.**

The final step in any shot is to accept the results for what they are . . . not for what they could have been. Accepting a result makes it easier to put closure on the shot you have just hit. Accepting and releasing the outcome from this shot affords you the freedom to move into the next shot with a fresh perspective and commit fully to that shot.

Adhering to these five basic strategies means you will give yourself the best opportunity to play one shot at a time with 100 percent commitment.

TAKE IT TO THE COURSE!

1. Commitment=pledge or promise. You are promising yourself that you are totally into the present shot. The shot you are facing is all that you care about . . . not the next one or the one you just hit, but the one you are over right now. You pledge your intent to commit totally.
2. Before you step into the ball to address and hit, commit yourself to the type of shot you want to hit, the shape of the shot that you desire, and the feeling of the swing that you want to execute; and finally, commit to the idea that your ball will go to the target.
3. Commitment is 100 percent. You do not commit a little bit . . . you either commit totally . . . or not at all!
4. Commit your eyes and body to the target.

(continued)

5. Commit yourself to the execution of a full swing or the motion that you have rehearsed from behind the ball in the preparation stage.

6. Finally, whatever happens, commit yourself to accept your result with a neutral reaction and to move on to your next shot with renewed vigor and enthusiasm.

FIVE

I Care Too Much About Score, Results, and My Reputation

*All men make mistakes, but only wise men
learn from their mistakes.*
—Sir Winston Churchill

I WIN—YOU LOSE

It is hard to comprehend that in today's world we need to have marketing programs that urge children to go out and play in vigorous physical activity at least sixty minutes a day to strengthen their minds and bodies. I highly support the program, but I ask, Do children really need a sales pitch to be motivated to go out and play? The concept is almost foreign to my senses. But, alas, times have changed, and so has the idea of physical activity and sport. However, a few things still remain the same, regardless of when you grew up. One of the most salient is the concept of "I win and you lose."

I grew up in a small town where I had a large number of friends who all enjoyed playing outdoor sports around my neighborhood. We used to play football, baseball, and basketball, sometimes all day. We would choose up sides and play sandlot battles that would often have scores as high as 80 runs in baseball and over 100 points in football. Talk about running up the score! However, at the end of a wonderful day spent hitting home runs or scoring touchdowns, we all knew who had won and lost the game. There were always definitive winners, and those who didn't win. If mine was the losing side, it wasn't that we really lost; we just ran out of daylight to create a comeback.

THE HOPE OF TOMORROW

It seems clear to me now that back then the score was important but it wasn't the absolute definition of success. What mattered was how you played the game and that you were a contributing member of your team. However, no matter when we played or who was playing, in our heads *we always knew who was winning and who was behind . . . we knew the score.*

The point was, if we lost, we would always have a chance to redeem ourselves in tomorrow's games. We always had tomorrow. I don't think we ever carried the label of *loser* around in our heads for long. The next day we would have a chance to be a winner, when yesterday's game would seem like a blur. We always played for the moment.

But I would only be kidding myself if I said that the score didn't really matter, because *it did.* The thought of being the best baseball player on your block gave you a feeling of being important. Or it could have been that because of your speed, you knew that when you had the football, no other kid could catch you. And it was especially nice if you were the first player chosen to play on an older player's team because of your reputation as a good hitter or shooter. Knowing that you had talent and being on winning teams helped instill a sense of personal mastery and confidence. The bottom line was that you were on the winning team and your score was higher than that of the guys you were playing. You went home to supper thinking, "I won and they lost!" Another day of challenge met with victory and satisfaction.

Now, I am not on a platform stating that winning builds character or that learning how to accept defeat gracefully is a vital ingredient for a well-balanced individual, but a final score does create a sense of objectivity and brings closure to a contested event. When you totaled up the score at the end of the day, you knew who had gotten the job done and who had failed to accomplish the game's objective.

Sport sociologists and psychologists have long argued pro and con about having scoreless contests in which every participant is declared a winner. Games of win-win help all to feel good about their participation and contributing effort. But in truth, even without scorekeepers or leaderboards, the participants in these contests intuitively understand who is doing well and who is falling behind. "How am I doing?" . . . "Am I winning?" . . . "Am I behind?" . . . are all questions we ask ourselves as we play these games.

In the result-oriented world of golf, you have eighteen holes, each with a par value, and you record your score as you play. The winner of the event is determined by the numerical outcome. In golf, the lowest scorer over the contested number of holes wins. Regardless of our age, we tend to revert back to our earlier understanding of sporting achievement as "I win and you lose." Therefore, questions of score and who is the winner prevail even in the friendliest of atmospheres, such as at your own golf club.

THE INEVITABLE QUESTION

I want you to imagine coming in from your round of golf with your regular foursome. You have had a pretty good day but it has had a few ups and downs. It has been a bit frustrating because you feel that you could have done a bit better, and you are feeling that you left a few shots on the course. (Don't we all feel like that to some extent?)

You are starting to leave your troubles and the missed shots behind you as you head to the nineteenth hole for a bit of banter and postround good cheer with your buddies. When you walk into the clubroom, you hear a voice from across the room loudly call out your name and you are asked "the Question": "Hey, what did you shoot?" You turn around and see one of your club members looking at you with a quizzical look on his face, and he asks you again, but this time in a a firmer and almost impatient tone, "Well . . . what did you shoot?!" Does this question and scenario sound familiar? It should, because almost everyone who plays golf gets asked this question. Almost inevitably you are asked your score when you come in from your day on the course. And the kicker is, it doesn't matter if you are playing in a tournament round or are just playing a few holes by yourself, you will still be asked "the Question."

Now, the Question may be framed in a number of different ways, such as "What did you fire?" "How was it out there?" "Did you go low?" "Did you tear 'em up?" These questions all mean the same thing, and you may be saying to yourself as you are reading this, Why is that? Why is it that people are always asking about my score instead of my interpretive response?

THE ROLE OF COMPARISON IN GOLF

People ask about your score for a fairly simple reason. They feel a need to compare how they measure up to others. In everyday life, we measure our job skills or what neighborhood we live in or what car we are driving to those of others. This is known as keeping up with the Joneses. We are always measuring our self-worth and success by how much or how little we have compared to others around us. This need to be more successful and to have as much if not more than others leads us to suffer from status anxiety. Status anxiety is what you feel as you strive to gain the respect of others by climbing the ladder of success, no matter what your ladder of endeavor.

Status anxiety also exists in golf. Other golfers want to know your score to determine if their round was acceptable. It is based on the concept of direct competition and the bottom line of "I win or I lose." For instance, if your score matches another golfer's score and he is considered a good player, you can take comfort that your total has matched his. If your score is lower than that of the good player, you take a certain pride in your day because you have played better than someone with a lower handicap than your own. If this player has a strong reputation in state and national tournaments, you think to yourself, If this person won all of these tournaments and I beat his score, that must mean I am pretty good. This accomplishment reinforces your status as a good player not only with yourself but with other members of your club or playing group. In essence, you have elevated yourself a bit in your club's pecking order.

But if your score is significantly higher than the good player's, you may feel disappointed because your play was far inferior to his standard. Many times this affects a golfer's self-confidence and golf esteem. Comparing our scores against those of others and even *our own expected score* provides us with a measure of achievement. We often use comparison as a measuring stick of our self-worth in other areas of our lives, and we learned to compare at an early age.

The bottom line is, others want to know not so much how your golf swing looks or whether you hit a number of good shots, but whether their score is lower than yours. They ask you the Question because they want to know how they did in comparison to you! The comparison is a mathematical score, an objective standard that is black-and-white! But the fascination with score is so prevalent in golf for another reason also, something I call the 99 percent factor.

THE 99 PERCENT FACTOR

When one team plays against another, one team wins at the expense of the other. There is a winner and a loser. The same is true for an individual sport such as tennis. I win by making you lose: I win my game, set, and match by scoring points and passing the ball by you without your being able to hit it back.

However, golf is not a direct-competition sport. The sport is played in parallel competition with all of its participants. All competitors are playing their own ball around the course, and your play does not affect another golfer's directly. That is, you are not defending or trying to stop other golfers from holing their putt (unless you yell in the middle of their backswing or something . . . and that is not done in the spirit of the game). At the same time, no one is trying to hold you back, either. So many golfers that I work with say that trying to "play my own game" is hard because they see what another player is doing and feel that they need to keep up or that they are so far behind that it is a losing effort so they start to "fold tent" and give up.

Golfers need to realize that those playing alongside them are not their true opponents or roadblocks to their golfing success. These are merely participants doing their own thing, alternating their time to hit with yours. Neither is it true that you are your worst or toughest opponent, even though many self-help golf books try to drive that idea home.

No, the one true opponent in golf is the challenge of the game itself. Golf is the most patient and befuddling opponent that you will ever face. The sport is played on a unique field of miles of obstructions and hazards, and you must send your ball into the hole with the entire world placed around it! But the real thorn is that golf has an ally. His name is Old Man Par. Par is the score that a scratch player would shoot over a course of eighteen holes and is the numerical measure that is placed on the scorecard. We are competing against a golf course and the par standard for which it is set up. Par scores of 70, 71, and 72 for eighteen holes are standard, and the only deviation is the number of par 3s, 4s, and 5s that make up the mix of eighteen holes.

However, a large majority of golfers—I like to call them the 99 percent group—measure their golf worth exclusively by the numbers on the scorecard. Even though we are playing for ourselves and personal achievement, the lesson that we learned from the backyard ball games, that to the winner go the spoils, makes it hard to let go of outcome thinking. Because we play parallel to other competitors, we still feel a sense of accomplishment when our score is the lowest in the group. We feel this when we are playing in tough conditions or on a course that has a high slope rating and where a low score is a numerical expression of mastery. We experience the feeling even more when we are engaged in tournament play with golfers of high repute and experience. Because we place so much emphasis on the score, we often lump our score and our self-image together: our score often reflects how we feel about ourselves and our golf esteem. If we understand our history and upbringing, we realize that we judge much of our success based on our standing with others. That is why we are fascinated with score. The winner of every PGA and LPGA tournament has the lowest total or objective score. It doesn't matter how the winner played or whether he or she truly deserved to win; the person at the end of the tournament with the lowest number of strokes taken . . . wins! That is pretty simple and straightforward.

Therefore, one of the greatest mistakes that players make is the inability to let go of the score and just get into playing their game. Because we place such a value on the bottom line, we forget that to have an effective bottom line, many times we need to let go of the numbers and outcomes and get into the actual playing of the game. For the 99 percent group of golfers, if they shoot good scores, they feel good about themselves, and that numerical factor is the all-important criteria for success. Although scoring low is the factor that we ultimately look at, it creates a vast amount of doubt, worry, and apprehension prior to and during a golfing round. The following stories from a number of players illustrate the mental mistake of worrying too much about scores, results, and how it may affect reputation.

THE MENTAL MISTAKE—I WORRY TOO MUCH ABOUT SCORE

"What did you shoot?" If you are one of the 99 percent golfers, you probably assume that your number on the card is the only measure that means anything. In reality, the score is only one measure of your performance, but when golfers start to predict their score or base their golfing confidence on their score, trouble may be on the horizon. Perry Swenson and Michelle Wie, both professionals on the women's tours, provide insights on how obsessive worry about score caused them to lose confidence and perform poorly. Perry Swenson:

I think my greatest mental mistake is that I just lost confidence to believe that I can play as well as I know I can play. Before college and when I was in college, I use to go out on the course and say to myself, "I am going to shoot a good score today, probably sixty-eight or sixty-nine," and then I would go out and do it, or come close to it.

But now, I have been losing my scoring edge, and so I go out now and say things like "I will be happy if I shoot seventy-six." I know that the edge in any golf performance is to have faith and believe that you can play well, but when you haven't had any success for a while, it becomes really hard to convince yourself that you can do it. Now I am getting back to the way I used to play, and hopefully my thinking will come around as well.

Perry's insights shed light on the many golfers who equate score with their golfing ability and talent. For example, if golfers play well and shoot a score that they expect, they feel pleased and their golf image is reinforced. However, if golfers go out and score poorly, they may feel discouraged or frustrated. This failure to meet their expectations leads to a drop of personal satisfaction.

Simply, if players score well, they like themselves. If they play poorly, they tell themselves that they stink and they feel worthless. If poor scores continue, their self-image as a competent performer is marred and the ability to remain confident is greatly jeopardized. Golfers need to learn the basic lesson that your score does not reflect you as a person or your creativity and worthiness. You are not your score! If you can identify with Perry and her statements, then you need to dismiss the scorecard and start to play the golf course shot by shot. When you say "I want to shoot this score today," you are setting up a scoring expectation. Then if you shoot that score, you will be satisfied. But any number higher than your target induces feelings of failure. If these feelings occur enough times, you erode your playing confidence and scoring ability. In short, you lose faith in yourself.

Perry talks about how early in her career she would tell herself to shoot a number and then go out and do it or at least come close. But after a while, the numbers strategy backfired and sabotaged her playing potential. Shooting scores that were higher than she expected eroded her confidence. When this happened, she started to bargain with herself and tried to adapt to the higher scores. Although she probably knew that she was a better player than her scores indicated, she did not know how to work herself out of her self-imposed slump. Allowing her scores to dictate her self-image as a player started the negative spiral that led her to believe that she was losing her scoring edge.

The critical mental mistake she made is that she set shooting a score as a goal, not seeing it as something that is created by playing the game one shot at a time.

Like Perry Swenson, Michelle Wie also placed some lofty scoring goals in her way, which interfered with her much-anticipated success. Unlike almost any other female golfer who has ever played the game, Michelle Wie needs little introduction to the golfing public. She is perhaps the most photographed and talked about player that has ever performed on the LPGA Tour. From the moment that she first stepped into the world of amateur and professional golf, Michelle was a star by virtue of her golfing talent and the prodigious length of her shots and spurts of golfing grandeur.

However, as the years went by and she failed to attain wins and live up to the media hype, she lost confidence, and many thought that she was just another failed prodigy. Michelle speaks of her mental mistake as having placed scoring and performance-perfection expectations on herself that held her back. By understanding her obsession and misdirected focus, Michelle corrected her greatest mistake.

I believe my greatest mental mistake is that when I was on the golf course, everything had to be perfect or at least I wanted things to be perfect. I was worried about executing the perfect swing and having everything go just the way I wanted. I probably placed too much emphasis on results and score, and when I didn't reach my goals, I became discouraged and lost a great deal of my confidence. I don't know why I was like that because off of the golf course I can chill and not take

(continued)

things so seriously and have to have everything "just so," bu I am simply too perfectionistic on the golf course.

When I would be at a tournament, I would even think about my pairings and my tee-off time and I would worry about all of that, and most of that was beyond my control, but I would still be overly concerned with the perfection aspect. I think part of that were the expectations that were placed on me by my-self and others, and I would feel sort of bad that I was not living up to my potential.

Now that I have matured a bit, I have realized that I don't have to be perfect nor should I expect myself to be, and I have taken a bit more of a laid-back attitude to the golf course and can now accept my imperfections and still play good golf. But, the expectation of being perfect or having to be perfect was probably my biggest mental mistake, and I am glad that I have learned that lesson and moved on. I am much happier now.

DR. BOB'S Rx FOR SUCCESS

Michelle wanted to have everything perfect or at least have the feeling that things would go perfectly, including her golf swing and score. With her overemphasis on results and score, when she failed to reach her goals, she would be discouraged and upset. Michelle felt she let others down when she wasn't doing well, and that led her into a deeper well of frustration and self-doubt. Ironically, Michelle is quite composed and laid-back when she is off the golf course. But when she stepped into the limelight of competition, she tended to be a perfectionist.

A few years back, I worked with Michelle on these issues, and we used on simplifying her process and letting the results take care of themselves. Instead of her trying to be perfect and over-control the golf swing and her results, we let the process take care of everything else. That included her swing, her results, and what others were saying or feeling about her. The task focus helped her get away from the "result consciousness" that overwhelms so many golfers that play the game, including Michelle. When you are thinking about too many things during your swing, worrying about your score, and pondering how you are letting yourself and others down, you are throwing a monkey wrench in the body's system. You simply collapse from too much mental overload. Having Michelle focus on doing one thing and only one thing, and doing it well, allowed her to get back into swinging to her target with a renewed trust, and good results have followed.

What we can take from Michelle's story is that wanting and striving for perfection just doesn't work. Wanting to hit the perfect shot and putt for the perfect score is impossible to attain and only leads to frustration and failure. However, focusing on the process and giving yourself permission to be human and make mistakes allows you to play to your real and developed talent. Adhering to a strategy that "this is what I can do but it is more than enough" provides a foundation for movement confidence and also allows you to not be so hard on yourself when bad shots or high scores occur.

FIRST AID FOR YOUR BRAIN . . .
DR. BOB'S Rx FOR SUCCESS

Here are a few things that you can do to help eliminate the "obsessive score mind-set" and to play with a one-shot mind-set free from expectations and thoughts of perfection.

1. First, you must dismiss the old lesson of "I win an ou lose" from your competitive past. Golf is not a ct competition between you and other players. Let the o r competitors play the 99 percent game. You need to s fresh with a new perspective. You need to become a percent golfer. Being a 1 percent golfer means that you ai focused exclusively on the shot at hand and you will tally the score *after* the round is over. Let go of being mentally handcuffed to the scorecard. Not thinking about the score produces a better score by virtue of your playing in the moment rather than playing the game of "keeping a running tally." This may be the ultimate paradox in all of golf because score (and keeping score in your head) is what everyone tends to obsess upon. This obsession constricts your freedom to play your game the way that you know you can play. To shoot lower scores, *you have to let go of wanting to shoot lower scores and understand that each shot needs to be counted at the end of the round.* While each shot counts, the players who are consistently winning and scoring low are the ones that make each moment and each shot count, not those counting and trying to predict their future score.

2. If you have been a good player and have scored well in the past, sit down and write out the things that you remember doing well. I imagine that you will find you had process activities going on in your mind rather than obsessing about how many birdies and bogeys you were making. A process activity means being involved in shotmaking, rather than projecting what you may score on the round or future holes. Examples of process activity include being visually engaged with the target, immersing yourself in your putting routine rather than labeling it a "must-make"

par putt, or just staying on task with the current shot. Staying committed to the physical task and staying in the moment for each shot provide a foundation of concentrated focus that keeps the counting demons from invading your playing focus.

3. Create a positive image of yourself and start saying a word cue about it to yourself repeatedly. For example, if you believe you are a tremendous competitor, say to yourself, "I am a ferocious competitor and no one at this tournament or in my foursome is a better player than me!" Reinforce something good about yourself and do it often. Remind yourself that you are a 1 percent player and that you are only concerned with the shot in front of you. Tell yourself often during the round that the only number that matters is 1. "One shot, one moment, one at a time" should be your new mantra. One of the most important pieces of research that has come out in the past ten years is that if you want to be competent, you have to start thinking and acting competently first, and the behavior will follow. Think, talk, and act in a one-shot manner and the scores will go lower by virtue of your new attitude and philosophy about the game and keeping the score.

TAKE IT TO THE COURSE!

1. If you want to shoot lower scores . . . you must let go of wanting or trying so hard to make a low score! Quit

(continued)

looking at your scorecard and the leaderboards. Y
must create and accept a "one at a time" mind-set.

2. Good scores happen as a result of your staying com
mitted to playing one shot at a time and staying involved with the task at hand...versus keeping a
running tally of your scorecard in your head. Remember, there are no good shots or bad shots...they are
simply "shots" that are tallied at the end.

3. Remember the mantra "One after one until I am done!"

4. Quit labeling putts as "par" or "birdie." A ten-foot putt
is just that...a ten-foot putt...regardless of the tally
of your hole score. The physical task is the same...it
is our perception of the event that changes. Stay on
task and realize that the execution of the shot is most
important...not the result.

5. Let others and what they may think of you go. You cannot control them...they cannot control you either!
Play your own game and get involved with doing your
best by beating the golf course—not your opponent.

6. You are not your score. Realize that your talent and
shotmaking are not evaluated by a simple addition at
the end of a round. Feel good about your process...
not a mathematical tally!

SIX

I Worry About What Others Think (About Me)

While one person hesitates because he feels inferior, the other is busy making mistakes and becoming superior.
—HENRY C. LINK

THE FEAR FACTOR

Perhaps nothing is more disconcerting or creates more performance anxiety than to have strangers and notable observers watch you do something that requires skill and concentration. This is especially true when you are on the first tee hitting your opening ball, and especially if you are not comfortable playing in front of others in the first place. The worry and doubt that precedes the actual hit is excruciating for many golfers. Even on the professional tours, a few of the best players in the world have told me that one of their greatest fears in a Major Championship is to top the ball off the first tee and then hear the crowd laugh at their mishap.

Not that this happens regularly but their remarks reveal that even the mentally hardiest of golfers experience jitters under the scrutiny of a watchful audience. Why does playing golf in front of others (whom we will probably never see again in our lives) create so much fear and doubt? The answer comes directly from the fear and anxiety literature. A strong correlation exists between the fear of social evaluation and hitting a golf ball when others are watching.

During my early years of psychological training I found that delivering a speech in front of strangers is the most mentioned item when people list their fears. Death, the loss of a spouse or loved one, divorce, and spiders all followed public speaking as the most mentioned of people's fears. Wow! That finding made me sit up and take notice. But let's think about that finding for a minute. If people consider getting in front of others and giving a public speech more fearful than encountering one's own death or losing a loved one, what makes them so scared? Here are some items that contribute to the feelings of fear when giving a public presentation or being in front of others:

Feelings of FEAR Related to Social Evaluation Anxiety

1. The fear of appearing incompetent

2. The fear of embarrassing oneself or one's family

3. The fear of evaluation and censure

4. The fear of humiliation

5. The fear of not meeting expectations . . . your own and others'

6. The fear of looking stupid

7. The fear of being laughed at or the brunt of others' jokes

8. The fear of failure or being unsuccessful

9. The fear of making mistakes

10. The fear that others won't like you

11. The fear of not measuring up or being as good as someone else

12. The fear of not getting what you want

This is only a partial list of the things that make people fearful of standing in front of others and giving a presentation. Do any of these items sound familiar to you when you are on a golf course and playing in front of others? Do you get nervous when you are on the first tee and strangers and other golfers are watching you and feel that they are judging you? Don't feel alone because almost all have these feelings when they play golf socially or in tournaments.

THE TRUTH OF CONFUCIUS

In public speaking, being in front of others and discussing your ideas and feelings places you in a vulnerable position of being judged and even rejected. You have to live with the consequences of your actions . . . there is no escape or closure upon giving a public presentation. The sense of personal fragility and being judged creates an enormous strain on one's psyche and self-esteem. The thought of being perceived as stupid or inept leads many people to fear speaking up and expressing their thoughts. Not only do they fear giving a speech in front of others, but they are continually reliving and rehashing the devastating failures of past presentations. Perhaps this is why Confucius, the wise Chinese philosopher, once said, "It is much better to remain silent and be thought a dolt than to open one's mouth and remove all doubt."

Many people view public speaking as a platform to reveal insecurities and lack of competence. If they do not deliver their presentation successfully, they reinforce feelings of inadequacy and ineptitude. Couple these feelings with past poor performances and you end up with people experiencing emotional death every time they are in front of an audience. Talk about your ultimate stage fright!

SOCIAL EVALUATION AND GOLF PERFORMANCE

If we link this example to the sport of golf, we find that the same intense focus on our athletic performance is much like in our giving a public speech. If you examine the different fears previously listed, you'll see that these are the same fears we have all experienced on the golf course. Golfers commonly fear making mistakes, looking stupid, or embarrassing themselves with less than stellar performances. For many golfers, the most important aspect of the game when others are watching is to hit the ball and get down the fairway with as much haste as possible without hurting their ego or reputation. Their main focus is to hit the ball away from the crowd and get into a place safe from prying eyes. This can happen on the first tee or even when a group wants us to play through them.

Think about this: How many times have you been waved to come through a group and you worried about what the other golfers might be thinking about you as you were playing your ball? The golfers that I have observed tend to rush and hit shots poorly just to get out of the way. I think the root cause isn't simply the desire to keep things moving, but rather a nagging feeling that other golfers are watching and evaluating every move. In a sense, an "inspection by others" is going on within people's heads. This awareness of others stirs up feelings of evaluation anxiety, which leads to swing tension and poor shots. The next time you play through a group and experience this phenomenon, remember this passage.

A classic example of a player who allowed others' opinions to affect her psyche is former women's collegiate player Christine Suchy. Christine was a solid player on two university teams and had a stellar junior career. However, she acknowledged that her greatest mental mistake was that she carried too much emotional baggage from focusing on other people's opinions, and trying to deal with the expectations of others, which affected her performance.

My number one mental mistake is more emotional than mental. I just can't let other people's judgments and evaluations affect the way I think and play. It seems that I am always worried about what a certain person will think or say when the round is done.

(*continued*)

I feel that I always have to play to a certain standard, and if I don't, I have to hear the "What's wrong with you?!" diatribe again and again. That is so sickening and discouraging. If I can just go and play my game the way I want to without all of the emotional baggage and expectations, I think that I would be a happier and better golfer.

WHO'S WATCHING ME?

As Christine's statement boldly suggests, worrying about others and what they may be saying about us while we are playing takes our focus away from playing our own game and doing our own thing. It is a harsh reality, but we are judged by our behaviors and our golfing performance. It seems as if all eyes are upon us. When you add that others may (or may not) be watching, you are adding an element of social evaluation, which many of us are not comfortable with. Being watched makes many of us doubt our ability, and we take our focus off hitting the golf ball and replace it with a debilitating energy called "Who's watching *me*?" This leads to the paranoiac thought of "Who's watching me getting ready to screw things up!"

A great example of this golfing paranoia is provided by Darin Tennyson, who was a general manager for the David Leadbetter Golf Academy (DLGA) at ChampionsGate for over fourteen years. Although not currently involved with instructional golf, Darin is still an avid student of the game. Because of his administrative workload and his tending to the various needs of the DLGA instructors and support staff, he hardly had a chance to play as much as he would have liked. Darin revealed his anguish with this revelation about playing golf with new clients and friends:

> I think my mistake is that I just want to get the shot over with and move on. I tend to rush and hurry myself when playing in front of others, and especially with people that I don't know or that I am playing with for the first time. I guess that I know from past experiences that I need to take more time to get the shot right in my head before I step into the ball, but that is easier said than done.
>
> I know what I should do but I end up hurrying myself anyway. I know that it is caused by worrying about what other people think of me, but I want them to think I can play well, but the more I think about them, the worse I become. I know it's a bad situation but I don't really get a chance to play very much, and when I do, the same thing happens all over again.

The anxiety that Darin feels is common for millions of golfers and is representative of a self-created anxiety spiral that spins out of control until Darin's round is either ruined or damaged, not to mention his golf confidence. He specifically mentions that based on his experience, he knows what he "should" do, which is to take his time and become comfortable and hit the shot as well as he can. But he ignores his own instruction and ends up hurrying himself anyway. Because he is doing this, he has made one mistake on top of another! He should have taken the time to acknowledge that he isn't ready and to back off the ball and get properly set. Then, after knowing that he is set and ready to go, can he proceed into the shot knowing that he is ready to execute with conviction.

However, because of the social-evaluation anxiety and just wanting to get the shot over with, Darin hastily ignores his inner voice of logical thought (which I will label Composure) and listens to another voice that shouts, "Let's get it over with . . . and quick!" This second voice (which I will call Anxiety) is more emotionally driven and impulsive. The second voice we hear directs our focus to be aware of others. When we listen to this impulsive voice of Anxiety, our actions are quick and our execution skills are lessened. If we listen to our Anxiety voice of fright and impulsivity and fail to acknowledge our Composure voice, we often find ourselves executing shots poorly. When we become aware of the internal noise of Anxiety, we must step outside ourselves and take the time to let the noise pass and get into our Composure state of calm and focused attention.

Because Darin chose to listen to his Anxiety voice and rushed, he committed another mental mistake, worrying about what the others thought of him rather than focusing on his game. This led Darin's focus into areas beyond his control. The results of this type of Anxiety focus are hardly ever efficient or productive.

YOU GOTTA LET GO!

The core issue that affects Darin Tennyson, Christine Suchy, and millions of other golfers is that they place more value and energy into what others are thinking about them than into their own shot! This misdirected energy creates worry and doubt. When you start to care more about what others are thinking about you than what you think about you, your misdirected mind can only lead you to trouble.

The grim reality is that oftentimes other players whom you are paired with don't care about what you are doing or how you are getting it done. What you may think someone is saying or thinking about you may not have any basis of truth. It may not even be happening at all! It is perhaps more of an idea in your head than in theirs. Let go of the paranoia.

Because we are narcissistic in our own golf game, we tend to overinflate our importance to others. In truth, no one cares about your golf game! Because other golfers must wait their turn to hit, their focus may turn to you to hit your shot before they can move into theirs. Alicia Stauffacher, a former collegiate player at the University of Northern Kentucky, discussed her greatest mistake, which reinforces the idea of letting the opinions of others go and staying true to your own game.

My number one mistake used to be that I didn't think that I had the physical tools and talent to compete with the other players. I don't know which came first, believing in myself more or just knowing that I had the confidence to play well and shoot better scores.

But I do know that if you let what others think of you get to you, or you worry too much about what they may or may not say about you, you are in trouble. So, I guess the biggest thing that has helped me is to just realize that you need to put everyone else's opinions about you away and just stay focused on yourself. After all, that is what really matters anyway.

Just for fun, the next time you play and are about to hit, look up quickly and notice what your playing partners are doing. Are they hawking or staring at you? Do they appear to be judging whether you are staying committed to your routine? I seriously doubt it. Most golfers are simply happy to wait for you because they are busy getting themselves ready for their shot! The key to this is to simply let others and their opinions, evaluations, and behaviors go. The ability to let go of the evaluations of others or what they are doing is paramount to your success. This is the basic premise of playing your own game to the exclusion of others around you.

WHAT ARE OTHERS DOING AROUND ME? ARE THEY TALKING ABOUT *ME*?

If you need more testimony that worrying about what others may be thinking and doing is a major issue, let's take a look at a great LPGA player from another decade and examine this common mistake that she admitted to making—and often! Australian superstar LPGA golfer Jan Stephenson admitted that worrying about others and not taking care of her game was part of her greatest mental mistake:

> The mental mistake I make or a mental challenge to my system is that I have always worried about what others are doing around me, and I have always felt that I need or needed to do something extraspecial. What I should have done and still
>
> (continued)

don't do is to forget about the other players and just play my game and not try to force anything or to press. It is just a part of my nature to always be aggressive, and I just feel like I have to go for it all of the time.

Even today after discussing this, I still haven't figured out how to deal with it. I still press and feel that I have to go after it. I don't know, but it is just how I am with everything. A high achiever or go-getter, I am always being very aggressive and going after what I want.

As Jan freely admits, it is hard to let go of worrying about others and to just do the things you know you can do. Jan even admits that she still doesn't always follow the dictum of "play your own game" and it still puzzles her! Because we want to play golf so well, we end up pressing, and in trying to stay ahead of others around us, we are always trying to get more out of our game, and this takes us out of our personal zone of control.

PGA Tour professional Bob Lohr also discussed his preoccupation with worrying about others and how it created problems in his development. Only when he finally realized that he needed to let go of others and what they might be thinking of his game did he start to develop personal control and play better golf.

Many times I would be worried that if I did step off and start over, my playing partners would think poorly of me or I would be having timing issues [taking too much time for a particular shot], and so I would just go ahead and hit it.

(continued)

> I finally decided later in my career that I wasn't going to worry about other players or what they thought about my taking my time, and I was going to make the commitment to myself from that point on that I would not play a single shot that would become sabotaged by doubt, hurrying, or poor planning.

Great players such as Bob Lohr and Jan Stephenson know intuitively that it is imperative to let go of others' evaluations and speculations, and the greatest players of all time focused exclusively on themselves and shut out everyone else around them. This is known as being in your "golfing cocoon" or your golf "bubble." Dominant players such as Ben Hogan, Jack Nicklaus, and Tiger Woods have all been known for their steely focus and their shutting out of the world when they are over a shot. This is what you need to understand about the power of the present moment . . . when you are totally into the shot and the moment, nothing else exists except you, your ball, and your target. Letting go of all of the external distractions, such as the watchful and evaluative eyes of others, is a major step to getting into your own "zone of optimal focus."

DR. BOB'S Rx: LETTING GO OF EVALUATION ANXIETY

Here are a few suggestions to enable you to stay focused on your own game rather than the assessments of others.

1. First and foremost, remember that the day is all about *you*. This is your time, your dollar, and your day on the

golf course. It is time that is invested in you! Set a top priority of being good to yourself for the entire day. Just as you remind yourself to have a proper setup, you need to remind yourself that you are playing for you and not for the entertainment or scrutiny of others. Being a bit more *me* and *target* absorbed rather than *them* absorbed is a positive step toward good golf.

2. If others are watching you as you step into your shot, remember that your focus should be on the target . . . *because the target is where you want your golf ball to go!* If you find yourself thinking about other players or past poor shots when someone was watching you, you need to *stop* . . . *back off* . . . and *reset* your focus. It is so important that you do not feel silly or that you are taking too much time. You are using only a few seconds, and it is much better to use a few seconds in this process than to hastily hit a shot and spend the next ten minutes trying to find a lost ball!

    Look out to where you want the ball to go and swing to that target. Use a descriptor word that describes your target and say it to yourself. For example, if the target is the right side of the fairway and a brown bush is directly on the sight line to the target, recite the words *brown bush* as you are stepping into the ball. Reciting an internal audio cue such as *brown bush* with a visual stimulus will keep you in the present and not let your mind wander into thinking about others or being aware that they are even present. The key is to stay in the visual present with a specific target focus. When you allow your attention to drift to others and what they might be thinking or saying, you have wandered into a realm of nonspecific information. That is, your mind can go anywhere, and that is usually where the ball ends up . . . anywhere but your intended target. Pick a specific visual target and swing to it!

3. It is vital that you have a basic understanding about human nature. People are curious, and they satisfy their curiosity by obtaining visual information and making decisions for themselves. For the majority of humans, "seeing is believing." Golfers will want to look at others and compare themselves to the object of their attention. Their focus is not about *you* as much as it is about *them*. The sooner that you can accept this, the easier it is to move on. If people are looking at you, you must make a conscious decision to recognize their wonderment and then to move on and get into doing your task, which is to hit your golf ball at your intended target. The sooner you can accept this as a truism for life, the sooner you remove the fear of possible embarrassment or of critical judgments of others.

4. For many golfers who suffer because of "curious onlookers," it isn't that their golf games are inferior, but that they handicap themselves with the *anticipation* of failing because people are watching them. To counter the feeling of possible failure, it is vital that you have an established preshot routine that has structure and rehearsed components that run off efficiently and keep you in the moment. Most golfers deviate from their routine and start to do things differently or at a different pace or rhythm when others are watching. Stick to your routine as if it were a fire drill. Maintain order and focus with the specific task of the rehearsed swing of the shot to your target. Adhering to your preshot routine helps your mind and body to be absorbed in a present and

action-filled mind-set rather than one that is vacillating and thinking about possible disaster.

5. It is critical to remind yourself that the majority of golfers who are watching you don't care whether you get off the first tee well or not. Their interest is their own game. You control you. That is the only thing you can control . . . but with that you have total control over how you make use of your time, how you structure your routine, and which targets you choose to fire at. You also have total control of your game and how you want to play. Do not let the evaluations or thoughts and words of others creep into your mind and start to create mental chaos. Let go of trying to control others. It is pointless and wastes a lot of your energy that should be directed to taking control of the things that are important to you . . . such as your shot and the target.

6. As in all things in life, the more times that you do something, the more you tend to feel composed doing it. This is somewhat akin to desensitization, which is to be gradually exposed to something noxious or distasteful until you become familiar with it and the distaste starts to dissolve. It is similar to becoming comfortable with being uncomfortable . . . at least for a short while. By exposing yourself to public evaluation on the practice range or by playing with strangers more frequently, the noxious element of possible embarrassment tends to pass. If you suffer from first-tee jitters, the next time you practice, place yourself around others and warm up. By doing this often enough, the pangs of distress may start to dissolve and the worry of what others may think about you will drift away.

TAKE IT TO THE COURSE!

1. Remind yourself that today is *your* day. It is about *you* and *your game*. The only thing that matters is that you focus on successful execution of your shot. Adhere to your routine and get your mind into the task at hand.
2. Give yourself permission to let go of others. They don't care about you or how you play or what you score. Dismiss your paranoia and enjoy your time on the links. This does not mean that you have to be a loner or impolite . . . simply focus more on yourself than others.
3. On the first tee, focus your attention down the fairway and onto your target. Do not allow your eyes to drift into any crowd of people who may be watching.
4. Take a few deep breaths and also make some large warm-up swings. Taking a large warm-up swing helps to insure that you will make a complete turn away from the ball.
5. Give yourself a specific verbal cue about where you want your ball to go. For example, if you see a spot in the fairway where you want your ball to go, vocalize to yourself that you want the ball to go there. Privately vocalizing your target helps to insure that you are on task and your mind will not wander or drift.

SEVEN

I Expect to Play Perfect

*The only real mistake is the one from
which we learn nothing.*
—JOHN POWELL

THE PROBLEM OF PERFECTION

"I hit that shot perfect!" You are likely to shout that phrase when you hit your ball squarely and the white pellet takes off like a bullet to the target. You might also utter this follow-up remark: "Now, why can't I do that more often?" These two phrases seem to go together like salt and pepper shakers. You don't very often see one without the other. Perfectionism and golf are somewhat synonymous, but when you try to put the two together, it is like mixing oil and water. They appear to be similar, but they don't gel as well as one would think . . . there is always some separation issue.

Perfection and golf are similar, but dissimilar, because a great deal of motor precision and efficiency is required to hit a golf ball accurately to a desired target. The degree of consistency and precise contact required is microscopic and demands a high level of motor development and skill. But to play golf at one's best, you must also be willing to let go of being perfect and strive for excellence instead.

This complicated issue of combining mechanical efficiency with artistry to perform various shots on the golf course is best illustrated by Naree Song, a touring and teaching professional who has struggled with bouts of perfectionist thinking.

I think that my biggest mental mistake is not simply a mental mistake, but it combines the physical part as well. I think that I have made the mistake of working and devoting so much time to the technical part of the swing, and making that as perfect as I can, that I didn't put the time into working on how to hit shots during a tournament round. So, in trying to develop a great swing, I feel that I spent so much time doing the mechanical and technical aspects that I didn't place as much emphasis on the shotmaking process as I may have needed to do.

As I have gotten older and matured as a tournament player, and doing some teaching as well, it has given me a better perspective of what is important and that you need a balance between the two aspects: of building a base for a sound swing and to be able to hit the appropriate shots that you may need during a tournament round of golf. Too many people seem to get lost in developing the quest for the perfect swing and probably should be spending a reasonable amount of time hitting shots and learning how to play the game as well.

As Naree's remarks illustrate, the balance between developing a sound swing and being able to take that swing and create great shots when it counts during a round is paramount. She speaks of having put so much time into working on her game that she neglected the attention it took to create a great mind to play and score at golf. Even when players have a great swing, if they make a poor shot on the course, they feel that they need to go back to the range and work on it some more. The cycle becomes never ending because perfect golf does not exist.

The problem with perfection is that even when you achieve perfect form and hit perfect shots, you rarely appreciate the achievement. For most golfers who suffer from perfectionist tendencies, when they do hit a perfect shot, instead of relishing the feeling and enjoying golfing nirvana, they dismiss the wonderful feeling and say, "Well, that's the way it should be!" or "It's about time that I hit one well!" They expected perfection and attained it but had no joy or satisfaction from hitting the shot they labeled "perfect." They are not deriving anything from a perfect shot that can build momentum for the next shot. Instead, they are relieved that they finally hit one that matched their inner expectations.

When a golfer takes this type of attitude to the course, you have a golfer with lofty expectations who, even if he or she plays well, is rarely satisfied. When you expect to play perfect golf, you are swinging a double-edged sword: one side of the blade is that you can hit all of the great shots you want to hit; the other side of the blade is that you are never satisfied with your results! Even when you hit it perfect, you think to yourself, This is the way it should be! But that is not all. What you are really saying to yourself is, This is the way it *must be*! This puts so much pressure on yourself to hit perfect shots that you are forcing yourself into a no-win situation of playing the game of "It has to be perfect!"

What is crucial to your golfing psyche and the health of your golf game is to learn to ease up on yourself and let go of the perfection quest. It is vital that you can feel good about shots that are less than "perfect" but are "perfectly acceptable." The problem lies in how we perceive perfect golf.

THE PERCEPTION OF PERFECT GOLF

Perfectionism is pervasive in the golfing world. If you walk up and down the driving range or go onto the course, you are likely to see young golfers beating themselves up for hitting less than stellar shots. They see their heroes on television hitting perfect shots (or as close to mechanical perfection as can be expected), and they feel that they have to play like this to be considered good. What golfers young and old alike forget is that when you are watching the touring professionals on television, you are watching an elite group of players who are playing perhaps the best golf of their lives and some are having their best tournament of the year . . . and we subliminally tell ourselves that this is normal for all golfers, all the time. This is an absolutely bogus perspective. You are watching the best players on the planet playing the best golf of their lives.

This is not a fair comparison for playing great golf. Granted, it is spectacular. Many of the shots that these players hit are unimaginable for the common player. But if your life vocation is professional golf, your interest and time devoted to excellence raises the bar of performance quite a bit. For the majority of golfers who play recreationally, it would perhaps be a reality check if we saw our heroes miss a few short putts or watched them hit their tee balls out of bounds. Perhaps a better way to learn what is vital for great scoring is to watch the top players deal with their frustration and find ways to be effective and achieve the best score they can on an off day. What we tend to forget because we rarely see it is that half of the field has already gone home because they played less than stellar golf, but even they had great moments earlier in the week.

The basic question that I am posing is, Why do we put so much pressure on ourselves to play perfect golf? Why have we programmed ourselves to try to swing and look like the perfect golfer or to have perfect form? This is a huge issue for many golfers. The following sections help to explain the issues of expectations and perfection.

GOOD TO GREAT?

In 2001, author Jim Collins came out with the book *Good to Great,* and it instantly became a bestseller among the business self-improvement literature. At the start of the first chapter in the first line, Jim discussed the concept that good is the enemy of great. Not only was this a catchy phrase that hooked the reader, but it set the tone for delivering a powerful message. His position was that Western society has a number of good schools and perhaps a lot of good businesses, but few great ones. The dilemma was that for all of the good, there was not enough great. A basic point was that many people and companies spend a lot of time and energy trying to do all of the right things and find that with all of their fury to become great, they end up with motivated mediocrity. They churned their wheels with a lot of effort, but ended up with average or less-than-stellar results. For many, their results did not match their initial expectations about what they could be.

Jim revealed that the good companies that went on to become great had leaders who retooled their thinking and rearranged their management to produce the most effective results within their organizations. The key to all of this was to develop clarity and have the persistence to realize the right things to do and to continue to do them, while at the same time understanding the pitfalls that might be holding the organization back and to cut those behaviors out. Many of the companies that went from good to great learned from their initial mistakes and corrected those core issues. Identifying what works and what doesn't plays a key role in the growth toward greatness.

GOOD TO GREAT IN GOLF?

Great players apply this concept of clarity and persistence to golf. Successful golfers understand the right way to do things and also learn via trial and error the wrong way to do things. Persisting in those endeavors that create momentum and measurable progress is paramount for consistent and long-term success. So is the elimination of faulty procedures and programs that sap energy and detract from momentum. For some players, it may take a long time to get key issues straightened out, but a few eventually do and have success.

However, a large majority of good players never achieve the level of greatness to which they aspire. They end up looking around at others who have become successful and asking, "Why them and not me?" Perhaps you are one of those players who question their ability. Questions such as Do I have it? Am I the real deal? Why haven't I found success yet? When will it happen?

Millions of golfers ask themselves these questions, and many of them harbor no illusions about playing on the PGA or LPGA Tours, but they do dream of winning their club championship, reaching a single-digit handicap, or even beating their personal all-time low score.

This is the conundrum found in golf. It seems for every great player that you read about or see on television or even play with regularly, certainly hundreds more have as much if not more talent, but end up with careers that fall far short of their dreams. What happens to these players? Is it that they don't have the talent or the passion to persist? Or could it be that success is more of a crapshoot and only a few make it? The answer may be a ceiling effect that impacts us all.

THE LADDER OF SUCCESS

If you want to become great at golf, you first have to climb several steps on the ladder of success. There are no shortcuts or magical potions that will expedite the process. As with any craft that requires precision and skill, you have to take each rung of the ladder one step at a time. For golfers, time is both an ally and a demon. I have always liked what actor and director Sylvester Stallone said when he acknowledged his success in creating and writing the *Rocky* series. He stated that success for him and anything worthwhile takes about ten years! What that also means is that you must have a passion to pursue the dream in the first place. Without the passion, the motivation to persist will eventually fade. Sly Stallone had the passion to achieve his goal, and eventually he reaped the benefits of his persistence with acting and directing fame. He is also a serious student of golf and plays regularly with that same passion.

In golf, persistence toward the goal requires steps to be taken every day. However, for all of the work that you put into the game, the benefits that you reap may not seem equal to your input. If you look up and down the driving ranges of the world, you are likely to observe hundreds, if not thousands, of "driving range pros" looking for that indefinable swing of perfection. They spend hours upon hours trying to achieve a feeling of mastery and ultimate competence. For them, grooving a perfect swing is the key to playing great golf. Although swing consistency and movement competence are important, striving for mechanical perfection can be a monumental, frustrating task. A ceiling that stands in the way of our achieving greatness must be recognized. Whether it is real or imagined, one item stops us on our way to achieving success: the ceiling of self-imposed expectations. Expectations are self-created benchmarks that suggest something must occur or be a certain way for us to have success or meet a standard of performance excellence.

In golf, perhaps the "greatest" expectation that we create is that we have to be perfect in our execution of the swing. Millions of golfers believe that if you want to be good at this game, you must first achieve perfect golf motion so you can perform well on the course. Testament to this way of thinking is the number of radically different teaching theories and devices that promise their way of playing golf is the answer! Golf media, magazines, and websites all preach the gospel that great golf is about having the perfect club coupled with a player who has perfect form. Golfers are among the most fervid consumers of teaching aids and improvement devices of all who play sports, but believing you can achieve greatness via mechanical perfection is a false and misleading premise. Let me explain.

THE CEILING OF PERFECTION

More so than perhaps any other sport, golf is a highly specialized game that demands much in the way of precision, accuracy of motor skills, and the power of decisive action. Golf is a game where business power, social position, or money doesn't help much in sending a white orb to a target 225 yards over water to an island green. That end must be achieved through a concept known as personal sweat equity. Sweat equity is the compilation of time, movement, and energy that all come together through something we call purposeful golf practice. In golf, players practice long and hard to achieve swing and movement competency. Once you reach mechanical consistency and you start to have a modicum of success, you are not just mediocre, but perhaps pretty good. The tricky part now is to tweak your goodness into something that is extremely reliable and consistent. For many players, the idea of being great is also akin to being perfect. You hear players comment on a shot that is well executed, "I hit that one perfect!" But, what does that mean? How does one define "perfect" or "perfection" in a golf swing?

The problem with trying to be great is that we think we have to be perfect or that we "must" hit each shot with mechanical perfection. This leads to a ceiling of frustration because we can never achieve mechanical perfection, and by trying harder to achieve it, we eventually wear ourselves out trying to obtain something that does not exist! This search for perfection and the quest for greatness leads many players into a quandary of frustration and despair. A good example of this is revealed by former collegiate player Brandon Eberle, who articulates his frustration with the search for "golf's Holy Grail."

My main issue that holds me back is that I am always trying to make the perfect swing or at least have a swing that looks and somewhat feels like the perfect swing. During all of my years attempting to become a proficient player, I have been inundated with so many swing thoughts that when I am playing, the thoughts of having to be perfect take over, and I forget that the main task is just to get the ball from here to there.

When I am over the ball, my mind starts to race with all of these swing thoughts, and I end up hoping that my swing will send the ball to the target. But I think the cause of all of this is the never-ending quest to have my swing "just right," and this leads me to not trust whatever swing that I have. It seems that I am always searching for a perfect swing and I am never satisfied with a swing that works pretty well.

Brandon states that he is trying to make the perfect swing, or at least to make his swing "look" perfect. His quest for the perfect swing brings to mind the alley cat that is running around in circles trying to catch its tail but ends up frustrated, tired, and irritable! A lot of energy is being used, but the result is always the same—the disappointment of not having achieved the goal.

In Brandon's case, the goal of swing perfection caused him to focus on his swing rather than the target. All of Brandon's focus is self-aware and on the "feel" of what a perfect swing should be, rather than being on where he wants his ball to end up. This is certainly not a good mind-set for playing golf. It may be okay for hitting golf shots on the range, but not in real performance conditions! Just like the cat that chases its tail, Brandon is chasing an elusive goal that may never be obtained. The real damage that is caused by this obsession with perfection is that something that works is ruined or is overlooked and dismissed because it is not perfect. Brandon admits that with his quest for the perfect swing, he becomes inundated with swing thoughts. This type of mechanical clutter for perfection definitely interferes with your ability to trust yourself and your swing while playing on a course.

Consistent with Brandon's issue is that of PGA and Champions Tour veteran Dick Mast. Dick explains that his largest mental error is trying to be too perfect and overcontroling his swing to make it "just right."

The largest mental mistake that I have made in my career is getting out of sync and staying too long over the ball. This happens when I am trying to really hit a shot "just right" or close to perfect, and I get out of my flow or sense of fluidity in my routine. It is a sense of knowing that I have the right club and right shot planned, but when I am over the ball, I disrupt the natural rhythm of the shot and I either try to hit it a bit too perfect or I want to hit it because it is a big shot.

The mistake I think that I do is I just don't step into the ball like a foul shooter in basketball and aim and shoot. I step in and make it a bit too ready or a bit too "overcontrolling." I need to just stay in the flow of my routine and execute the shot. When I adhere to my routine and execute the shot in a state of rhythm and fluidity, I hit a lot of great shots and especially in pressure situations.

By trying to make sure that everything is perfect, Dick over-controls a swing that is better when allowed to run off automatically! When we coerce a swing rather than allow our brain's motor blueprint to run the show, the sense of rhythm and automation is compromised, which is not conducive for movement confidence or swing consistency. One swing is filled with force and a "trying" effort, versus one that flows automatically.

Brandon Eberle and Dick Mast share a common issue: they both try to play the game of "perfect golf swing." In trying to achieve perfection, they abandon a swing or a swing feel that is working. They sabotage their swing feel for one that feels more perfect or looks a bit more like the perfect swing. That is the double-edge sword of searching for perfection. When you have something that is pretty good and it is working and you have a bit of trust in it . . . why change? The dilemma comes when you feel that you can be even better and you opt to make the change. But by making a change and risking what was once working, you also put into jeopardy the notion of trust when you go play. A mental dilemma indeed!

YOU NEED TO CHANGE

A perfect example of changing for something that is "supposedly better" was presented earlier in this book by tour player Cameron Yancey. Cameron lost much of his confidence by trying to please other people rather than himself, and he got away from being Cameron Yancey. This even affected the way he would swing the golf club. Read what he says when he would miss a cut and how others would come up to him and tell him that in order to play on the tour, you needed to hit the ball a certain way. This constant suggestion of "you need to do something other than what you are doing now" eroded his confidence and ultimately his playing personality and individual style:

> For example, I normally draw the ball and I can control it very well. Well, when I got to the tour, there was just player after player who said, "You need to learn how to cut it. If you don't learn how to fade the ball, you will be done in no time."
>
> Well, I listened to those guys and what happened? I screwed myself up and lost the confidence in my playing ability because I was trying to hit the ball like everyone else and I am not like anyone else. I am Cameron Yancey and I need to play like Cameron Yancey.

We can learn from Cameron's plight that sometimes you have to take stock and realize that what you have is pretty good. But to go from pretty good to really good or perhaps even great, you may have to leave the comfort of good and venture into unchartered waters. Cameron's game was good enough for him to make it to the PGA Tour and also win several minitour events, and a draw was his dominant shot. Every touring professional seems to be constantly looking for an edge to help him or her improve because of the high level of competition. Many of them are continually learning how to control the flight pattern of the ball, its trajectory and overall distance. Year after year, with a bit of improvement in different areas, many of them make substantial gains in overall performance. Early in his rookie year on tour, Cameron became susceptible to the good intentions of others, who were offering advice on what to do with his game to take it to the next level. They repeatedly mentioned that if he didn't learn to hit the fade, then his days on the tour were numbered.

People give advice not only on the pro tours, but also at your home club. If you are playing with others and they see you are having trouble, it is only human nature for them to try to help.

I think golfers need to be cautious in listening to and accepting what others are providing. Golf advice is cheap and it seems that everyone has a secret to share. The belief is that if it worked for them, it will certainly work for you. This is when you must recognize the slogan "Buyer beware!" Why would you change something that is working, and why would you listen to others when you have developed trust in your own style? That is the million-dollar question. This is a classic example of having something good and wanting to turn it into something great. Often inevitably in golf, in trying so hard to become better, we end up going backward and losing confidence in what we once had.

BIG-TIME EXPECTATIONS AND PERFECTION

A prime example of someone who faced huge expectations from others and herself is Michelle Wie. One of the greatest talents in golf, Michelle reveals her mental mistake was that perfectionism was convoluting every area of her game. I have placed her quote here so that you can reread her mistake of placing pressure on herself to be perfect.

I believe my greatest mental mistake is that when I was on the golf course, everything had to be perfect or at least I wanted things to be perfect. I was worried about executing the

(*continued*)

perfect swing and having everything go just the way I wanted. I probably placed too much emphasis on results and score, and when I didn't reach my goals, I became discouraged and lost a great deal of my confidence. I don't know why I was like that because off of the golf course I can chill and not take things so seriously and have to have everything "just so," but I am simply too perfectionistic on the golf course.

When I would be at a tournament, I would even think about my pairings and my tee-off time and I would worry about all of that, and most of that was beyond my control, but I would still be overly concerned with the perfection aspect. I think part of that were the expectations that were placed on me by myself and others, and I would feel sort of bad that I was not living up to my potential.

Now that I have matured a bit, I have realized that I don't have to be perfect nor should I expect myself to be, and I have taken a bit more of a laid-back attitude to the golf course and can now accept my imperfections and still play good golf. But, the expectation of being perfect or having to be perfect was probably my biggest mental mistake, and I am glad that I have learned that lesson and moved on. I am much happier now.

We can learn from Michelle that unrealistic and perfection-ist tendencies are wellsprings of failure. Michelle freely admits that wanting to be perfect and have absolute control was her mental mistake. However, when we look back at her early career, we need to remember that in all of women's golf, never was so much expected from a player as from Michelle Wie. The comparisons of Michelle Wie with Tiger Woods were rampant, and with all of the media attention and endorsements deals, it must have been overwhelming for her. To counter the intense performance pressure, Michelle felt that she needed to be in total control of everything, including her golf swing. Neither she nor anyone else could fulfill her obsessive desire to have everything "just so." The only thing that is certain for people who expect perfection is that they will eventually meet failure and disappointment.

A major part of Michelle's perfectionism came from unrealistic expectations about how she needed to perform on the golf course. Because she is a statuesque athlete, Michelle was even given the nickname the Big Wiesy, similar to Ernie Els's moniker the Big Easy. Comparisons of this nature were the standard by which she was judged. Off the golf course, she is more laidback and things don't seem to upset her as much. This is perhaps understandable because off the golf course Michelle doesn't face the same sort of expectations for performance.

Another aspect of her perfectionism came from trying to match her golfing performance to the expectations of others. As human beings, we tend to let others down as they let us down. It is hard to live your life for someone else's wants and needs, let alone to match your own expectations. If you can imagine the burden of trying to play for others and not let them down, you can imagine the weight that Michelle must have felt for all of the media exposure and large corporate dollars that expected her to perform . . . and not only to perform well, but to win! For many golfers, the added burden of feeling that they have to play well for other people places a heavy strain on their shoulders. In college and professional-golf team events such as the Ryder Cup and Solheim Cup, players feel the pressure of not wanting to let their teammates down, and they speak openly about the burden they place on themselves.

The bright lining of Michelle's story is that as she has matured and endured the hardships of athletic injury and failure, she has learned to lighten up. Letting go of feeling that she had to be perfect provided her with a new attitude to play with confidence and emotional freedom. She is playing better golf by understanding that you do not have to be perfect to be successful. But the ultimate justification for Michelle, as for all "reformed perfectionists," is that she now is much happier on the golf course, which shows up in her attitude and her smile. Michelle's joy now comes from hitting great shots and enjoying the game, by not having to meet unattainable standards of perfection.

FALDO AND WOODS: GOOD TO GREAT DOES HAPPEN

This gray cloud of perfectionism does have a bright lining. Although extremely rare, outstanding athletes exemplify the grit and dogged determination needed to attain heights that most golfers can never imagine. Two players, from the past and present, are great examples of golfers who took what they had, which was already good, and turned it into something great. Nick Faldo and Tiger Woods changed something that was working well and opted for higher aspirations. Although they knew the gamble was great, they felt the eventual payoff would be worth it, and they were right.

The player-teacher duo of Nick Faldo and David Leadbetter started working together in 1985. After his professional debut in 1977, Nick played for several years with the hopes of the British Isles riding on his shoulders. Six foot three inches and with the looks of a Hollywood movie star, Nick was unsatisfied with his play over his initial years on tour, and the British tabloids were hard on him as well, tabbing him Nick "Foldo" for his inability to close the deal down the stretch. Nick approached David in 1985 and said, "I am tired of being mediocre. I don't care how long it takes, but I am willing to see it through and get better." Leadbetter told him directly it would take a massive amount of work, not just a few minor alterations, and may be as long as two years to see any real change. The rest is history. Two years later, David Leadbetter turned out to be a prophet, and Nick ended up winning six Major Championships and multiple tour titles while being a stalwart leader of the European Ryder Cup teams for many years.

A few years later, another young man with an impressive junior record and proven tour performance would be making a change as well. Upon winning the 1997 Masters with a record-breaking performance, Tiger Woods told his teacher, Butch Harmon, that he wanted to make some changes to his swing. Here was someone who not only won his first Major Championship, but set a new scoring record! Why would he want to change? Why fix something that wasn't broken and seemed to be working effectively? Tiger's thinking was that he could change a few things, and eventually, if he could implement those changes and feel comfortable, the sky could be the limit. It would not just be about winning, but dominating.

Butch Harmon told Tiger that if he had the commitment to pursue this avenue, it would take some time. Almost two years to the day after they initiated the swing changes, Tiger felt comfortable enough on the range to call Butch and let him know that he had finally arrived. The following year, in 2000, Tiger set a new standard for golfing performance and number of major victories. No one has ever had a record-setting season such as Tiger had in 2000. His vision of what could come from making those changes finally paid off.

We can learn from both men and their quests for perfection

that you must be patient, focused, and stay unerringly true to your course. You must pay the price of blood, sweat, and tears to make a major change. Both Tiger and Nick made that commitment to themselves and their coaches. Nick and Tiger also understood that in their quest for perfection and ultimate swing efficiency, they needed to master every mental issue that is mentioned in this text. These two individuals had extraordinary mind-sets with a passion for excellence that is as rare as the Hope Diamond. Few individuals have the mental and emotional makeup to do what Tiger and Nick have accomplished. It took both players at least two years to implement and feel that they had made the significant changes. Now, even after all of the years that they devoted to their games, they both insist that their game is about constant refinement and improvement. The quest for perfection is never ending.

The ultimate lesson that we can learn from Nick and Tiger is that in golf, if you want to see how great you can become, it is vital that you *strive* to be as perfect as you can. The problem is that when you *expect* to be perfect, you wind up frustrated and discouraged. That is, if you expect to hit your shots perfectly or don't feel anything positive from the endeavor, you merely set yourself up for failure. The key to golfing success is *striving to be as motor efficient as you can.* Motor efficiency and movement confidence are based on using your body to create the most fluid and solid swing that you can produce and then to accept the result.

This is what is meant by striving for perfection and pursuing golf excellence. In hitting a golf ball perfectly, if there isn't a positive feeling, then little momentum is created. The issue is, how do I create a feeling of motor effectiveness and rid myself of "perfectionistic expectations"? The following section will provide you with some ideas.

DR. BOB'S Rx FOR ACHIEVING EXCELLENCE

1. ***Change your perception***. To alleviate the pressure you feel from having to play perfect golf, you must first change your perception about what great golf is. Golf is not a game of perfect. It never has been nor will it ever be. Perfect golf does not exist. The perception is the problem. We need to develop a philosophy for playing excellent golf, not perfect golf. Excellence is a high standard and is attainable. Even the greatest golfers of their eras, Ben Hogan and Jack Nicklaus, agreed that when they were winning their tournaments, they would only hit four or five perfect shots during a round. The rest of their shots were less than perfect but were excellent or, at least, effective. Ben and Jack used an accepting philosophy that allowed them to strive for perfect, but allowed them to accept less than perfect but effective results. If this philosophy was good enough for Ben and Jack, it will work for you as well!

2. ***Use a different vocabulary***. If you are plagued by bouts of perfectionism and use the word *perfect* often in your golf vocabulary, it may be a good strategy to drop the word. You may want to replace it with words that have less emotional punch. The problem is that *perfect* is a hot-reactor word. Hot-reactor words may create feelings that are either too high or too low in emotional affect. *Perfect* is a hot-reactor word much in the same vein as *terrible* or *pathetic*. When you use *terrible* and *pathetic* to describe your golf shot or golf game, the reaction that you create

disrupts your emotional balance. When you use *perfect,* you are creating emotional imbalance as well, in the opposite direction. Try words that are cooler in emotional tone. When you say that a shot was *efficient,* you are referring to the solidness of hit and of your golf swing. When you use a cooler word such as *effective,* you are referring to the result. An effective result gives you a good chance to hit the next shot or make the next putt. By using other words than *perfect,* you are helping yourself to achieve mental and emotional balance, which is a vital key for consistent golf. It also helps to take pressure off yourself, knowing that you do not expect to be perfect.

3. ***Develop a different evaluation system.*** Instead of feeling that you have to hit your ball perfectly in order to feel good, you may want to use other aspects for your evaluation. Remember, if perfect is your performance standard, you are setting yourself up for failure unless you hit a perfect shot. Even if you do hit it perfectly, you do not create feelings of positive momentum because only perfect is acceptable. Instead of continually frustrating yourself with an unachievable standard, create a different value system. You may want to grade yourself on the feeling of solidness or committing to the core idea of what you wanted to do with the shot. For example, if you step onto the first tee and are having problems getting the ball into the short grass, instead of trying to hit the perfect shot that splits the fairway, focus on hitting the ball squarely. Step into the shot and remind yourself that when you create a full turn, it gives you a great chance of swinging freely to your target. After the shot, instead of judging it by whether it turned out perfect, grade yourself by the degree that you

allowed yourself to make a full turn back and through to your target. By creating a different value standard, you move away from an unachievable goal and toward a system that is continually reinforcing.

4. ***It's not how you drive, but how you arrive.*** Think of your golf game as driving a car. If you have to make it to the airport in an hour to catch your flight, does it matter what type of vehicle you drive or ride in that gets you there? The important point is that you arrive in time. Relating this to golf, the bottom line is that no one gives you a first-place check or trophy for playing perfect golf or having a perfect golf swing. If that were true, then Gene Littler, Tom Purtzer, and Adam Scott would have won every tournament in the past three decades! The important point is that winning golf is played with great shots, average and poor shots, and miraculous recoveries. A shot is a shot is a shot. No one shot is greater or less than any other. The total of all of these less-than-perfect shots is what separates the champions from the also-rans. Give up the idea of playing perfect and get into the thought of arriving at the finish line ahead of everyone else, no matter what type of golf vehicle you may be riding in!

5. ***Choose functional over fancy.*** Consistent with idea #4 is, it's important not how something appears, but its effectiveness. Remember that the golf ball or golf course doesn't care how something looks or feels. So many golfers make the mistake of wanting to hit the perfect shot when a less-than-perfect shot or ordinary shot will do just as nicely. For example, your ball is down in a small

depressed area and the grass is cut tight. You want to hit your sand wedge and open the face and execute a high flop shot because you have recently seen Phil Mickelson on television hit this shot perfectly during a Major Championship. Although you do not have this shot in your golf repertoire, you still want to hit it perfectly, like Phil. Take pressure off yourself and make the smart play and hit the shot that you know you can hit. If the smarter play is a bump-and-run into the hill, so be it. Playing the high-percentage shot that has less risk will almost always elicit more favorable returns on the scorecard.

TAKE IT TO THE COURSE!

1. Perfect golf does not exist. Let perfect go. Instead, focus your mind on hitting excellent and effective shots. Strive for perfection, but do not expect it to happen.
2. Do strive to be excellent to yourself and let good things happen as a result of your mind's being in the proper place.
3. Play the shot you know you can hit...keep it simple and effective. Choose functional over fancy. Remember, it is not how fancily a shot went into the hole; the important point is that it *made* it in!
4. Know that you will miss shots. Even the best golfers in the world miss shots. Accept the misses and move on. Change your self-talk from *a good miss* to *effective*.

(continued)

5. A shot is a shot is a shot. Play each shot with a consistent focus and do not label a shot good, bad, or indifferent. Your task is to get your mind and body into each shot with purpose and positive intent. The sooner you can do that, the sooner you will shoot lower scores and win tournaments!

EIGHT

I Think Too Much

*I've learned that mistakes can often be
as good a teacher as success.*

—JACK WELCH

HELMET FIRE—THOUGHT OVERLOAD!

I want you to clear your mind of any thoughts you might have right now. Go ahead. Clear your mind and think about nothing. I will wait for you. Don't read. . . . I am serious. Start now. . . . Clear your mind.

Stop! Welcome back. Was your mind clear? It's hard to do isn't it? Well, think about this: it is virtually impossible to clear your mind entirely because it is always processing information. Consciously or unconsciously, your brain is always working. Every second of your life you are being bombarded by your sensory systems, providing information on what you should attend to or be aware of. Most people don't realize that every waking and nonwaking minute of your life you are thinking about something . . . even if you don't want to think! Even while you are sleeping, you are still having thoughts that produce pictures inside your head that stimulate your body and make it feel tense, sweaty, and achy. No wonder we never get a good night's sleep!

Neuroscientists suggest that a mature human being may have as many as sixty-six thousand thoughts in a day. If that is true, for every hour that you are alive, you are processing 2,750 thoughts. Since an hour has sixty minutes, you have 45.8333 thoughts per minute. Since a minute has sixty seconds, you have 0.763888 thoughts per second. That is roughly a thought per second your entire life! Whew, it makes me mentally tired just talking about it.

Out of this constant barrage of thoughts, we respond to some and simply filter out or discard others. If we didn't have this capacity to filter out information, we would be on overload. For example, in the military, when fighter pilots put on their helmet, they have multiple computer weapon systems reporting within their headgear. As they are flying at speeds of upward of Mach 2, they are constantly monitoring reports from their helmets, watching the controls inside the cockpit, and scanning the sky. When their information systems overload, pilots call it helmet fire. The human brain cannot handle this deluge of information.

Helmet fire is also termed task saturation. Task saturation for a fighter pilot is having too much to monitor. Similarly we can have too much going on inside our heads when we play golf. Although we do not don headgear with systems monitors and we do not have SAMs being fired upon us (though every now and then we do have to monitor the sky for a wayward shot when someone yells, "Fore!"), we still have task saturation.

HELMET FIRE AND GOLF

Golf is the ultimate thinker's game because you can use your mind to provide you with an edge to compensate for other areas of your game where you may be a bit deficient, such as in power and distance. For example, on a long par 5, if you do not have the physical ability to reach the green in two, you can think through your second shot to leave you with a comfortable distance for your third shot. Giving yourself a good "leave" for your third shot optimizes your chance for hitting it close and making birdie. By thinking the shots through, you can negotiate your way around the golf course and create an edge for yourself over Ole Man Par.

But there is a problem with thinking too much. To be effective on the golf course, you have to know when to think and when to stop and take action. For many golfers, this is a huge problem not only in playing the game, but learning how to swing the club effectively. Millions of golfers struggle with not only where the ball needs to go, but also have an internal battle about how they will swing the club to hit the ball. According to my friend and world-renowned swing instructor David Leadbetter, this debate prevents players from ever reaching their true potential.

I believe the biggest mental mistake that I see most players make is that they are overloaded with too much conscious thought when they swing the club. They try and overcontrol the swing rather than trust their swing and go play. The golf swing should be instinctive rather than manipulated or

(continued)

forced. I see players who just get in their way by having too much conscious thought and ruin their motion that by all means should be instinctive and reactive.

The swing should be guided by a subconscious mechanism that takes over, and that is why you practice so long and hard, for those subconscious tendencies to take over and allow you to swing freely and instinctively from what you have trained versus trying to force something and become flooded with self-instructed thought.

If you think about your game, reflect on how many times you have been over the ball and tried to instruct yourself. You were giving yourself verbal orders to carry out a motor program that was probably overloaded with component parts. I would imagine that it was rather hard to swing with naturalness and fluidity because you were making a golf swing that was coerced rather than a swing that ran off automatically without conscious interference or instruction. This is exactly what David Leadbetter is talking about when he states that many golfers ruin a perfectly acceptable swing motion with a lot of conscious directions about how to swing the golf club. By verbally giving themselves orders during the swing, they overload the motor function of the brain. The swing that is produced appears manipulated, robotic, and less than efficient! Not a good combination for any golfer.

KEEPING IT SIMPLE

Having too many thoughts during your swing can only interfere with the execution of what should be a well-rehearsed and developed motion. Filling your mind with too many technical thoughts can complicate things, especially if you make your living playing golf, as touring professional Robert Damron reveals in the following statement.

My greatest mental mistake is that I have too many things going on in my head. Mostly, I have too many swing thoughts. I am a feel player, and when I have too many swing or mechanical thoughts going on in my head, that's not me or my style of play. So, right now, I would say that my greatest mental mistake is not sticking with one swing key or swing cue and jumping around and trying too many swing thoughts.

Too many and you don't know which one to use or which one will work. I just want to keep things simple, and when I don't do that, well, it's just a mental mistake and I know better than to make the game too complicated.

I mean when I played with Arnold [Palmer] he told me that when he played his best, it was that he only had one thing in his head that was simple, which allowed him to just hit it and chase it. That's where I need to be, just one thing and go. When I do that, I usually do pretty well.

For Robert, keeping things simple is how he plays his best golf. When he focuses on too many things, he ends up confused and strays from his natural athletic ability. He speaks of being a feel player, and for him, a major mistake is to try to become too mechanical with an overload of technical information. He speaks of playing with Arnold Palmer, who said he kept things simple, such as having only one thought, and stepping in and hitting it and then finding it and hitting it again.

Robert's vital revelation is to do one thing well. When he jumps from one swing key to another, he knows he is making a mental mistake. For him, less is certainly more. "Less" means less conscious instruction and *more* reliance on what he has trained and overlearned via years of repetition and practice. Robert focuses more on his swing feel and less on technical keys to stay true to his style of play. By cutting out all of the extraneous "swing fat," he is better able to just go play and simply hit it and chase it. Doing one thing and sticking to it provides him with more swing confidence.

CLEAR THE MECHANISM

Like Robert Damron, other players try hard to clear their minds and to get into the moment. However, the constant chatter within their heads doesn't allow them much peace to focus on the ball and make a good stroke. By having too much going on inside their brain, they not only create inefficient movement but suffer the emotional consequences of hitting poor shots, which creates a negative downward spiral. One extreme example of a player who is attempting to make sense of the internal chatter is former University of Florida collegiate player Ornelle Nouveau. Ornelle says her greatest mental mistake is having sporadic thinking, which leads to poor shots and emotional fallout.

My biggest concern is that I am all over the place with my thinking. I have so much doubt about where the ball needs to go and where it might end up. I don't have any answers about how to stop it. . . . I guess that is why I play the way I do

(continued)

sometimes. . . . I am just filled with doubt and anxiety about the consequences that usually end up poorly.

When I play well, I still tend to doubt a bit, but not as much. But all it takes for me to start questioning my ability or my swing is one bad shot. Then, I try to figure out what it was that caused me to hit that shot, and then I am working on my mechanics, and that starts me to doubt even more. It's awful to feel this way.

Ornelle's dilemma is shared by millions of golfers. As she is stepping into her ball, she is unsure of what might happen. She is focusing her mental energy on all of the negative possibilities. Ornelle suffers from golfer's helmet fire coupled with high result expectancies. That is, she invests so much of her mental energy into what might happen with the shot before she hits it, she creates an emotional expectancy based on the outcome of that shot. This excessive worry leads her to doubt her ability and eventually produces bad swings. Not only does her thinking go adrift, but the poor shot creates emotional turmoil that she carries into her following shots. When a player suffers from too much thinking, every element that is discussed within this book comes into play. That is why it is so important to cut out all of the extraneous fat from your performance and learn how to focus your mind on a single element for ultimate golf performance.

Ornelle says that all it takes for her to create a downward spiral is one poor swing. This is what I label a one-shot destructive mentality. The fallout from this single shot creates an inner turmoil of how to fix the swing so that it doesn't happen again. An internal alarm goes off in a golfer's head that says, "We need to fix this thing and gain control . . . fast!" This fix-it mentality then leads to conscious swing instruction, which leads to tightness and lack of trust in the swing. What may have started as a simple physical error has now turned into a cognitive and emotional quagmire.

TWO MISTAKES THAT STEM FROM OVERTHINKING

Ornelle has made two mental mistakes even before she swings the club. Her first mistake is that she does not have a clear plan about how she is going to execute her shot. This is the fundamental reason her thinking is all over the place. She has no direction for her performance and no clear targeting strategy. She is searching randomly for an answer that will never reveal itself. The second mental mistake is that she is absorbed in result thinking. Her thoughts are not about execution in the moment, but are entirely directed toward the result. By worring so much about the consequences of her shot, she creates tension and self-doubt before even stepping into the ball. With this type of mind-set and mood-set, it is little wonder she has problems hitting the ball squarely to her target.

WHERE DID THAT THOUGHT COME FROM?

Ornelle is not alone in having misdirected thoughts and feelings on the golf course. Even veteran tournament winners suffer the same maladies of misdirected thinking and skewed thoughts. PGA and Champions Tour professional Hugh Biaocchi spoke to me about his greatest mental mistake, and it sounded familiar indeed.

My biggest mental problem? I think it all starts with clutter. The clutter in my head is going on all of the time. It is hard for me to quiet my mind, and I constantly have chatter, noise, or whatever you call it going on in my head, and I just try and get it to calm down, but it is a really tough thing to do. I try and focus and be in the moment, but I find it hard because of so much other stuff that springs into my mind. I have so many questions that often enter my head at the wrong time... things such as what is the cut going to be? Or, is this the right shot that I want to play?

There are always new thoughts coming in, and if I can just quiet my mind, then I seem to play really good golf. In fact, it becomes relatively easy. I realize that great focus is really important, but it just becomes hard for me sometimes because I have so much other stuff from all around me that enters in and takes me from a great focus to one that is scattered much of the time. I have a lot of stuff and it just comes in. The task for me is to allow it to pass or to just block it out. It is hard, but it can be done.

Hugh's inability to focus on command brings up a great point that every golfer can relate to: *I know what I am supposed to do; it's just that I don't do it!* Most golfers know that it is important to focus on a single task when they step onto the golf course. They also know intuitively to be singularly focused in the here and now, to play one shot at a time. But it is much easier to talk the talk than it is to walk the walk! Hugh, like so many other great golfers, is forthright in his admission that his mind wanders, and with so much going on around and within him, he finds it difficult to block out all of the extraneous information.

When you are playing well, it is easy to be locked on your target and to stay within your own little bubble, but other times it becomes virtually impossible. This is a human problem. We are programmed via evolution to process incoming information to alert us to any external dangers, but in the midst of all of this reception, we may become overloaded with too many things at once.

Hugh notes that when he is playing, a random thought will enter his mind at the most inappropriate moment, such as "What is the cut going to be?" or "Is this the right shot that I want to play?" The key is to know what to focus on and what to dismiss from your awareness. It is much better to let bits of extraneous information pass rather than to fight them off via willpower, which has little effect anyway.

THE IRONY OF *DON'T*

As golfers, we tend to say the word *don't* to ourselves so often that it becomes a negative earworm while we play. An *earworm* is a pop psychological term given to a sound, song, or word that gets stuck in your head and won't leave your conscious awareness. An example is when you hear a song or a jingle on the radio and you find yourself whistling or humming the melody the entire day. That is the fundamental aspect of an earworm. It gets into your head and stays there for a long time until another thought or earworm replaces it.

One of the most common earworms in golf is a piece of paradoxical instruction that you have probably used or heard a million times: "Don't go there!" This is probably uttered to you by your caddie, friends, playing partners, or even yourself as you bark out orders to yourself telling you where you do not want your ball to go. However, by telling yourself *don't,* your mind gravitates toward a seductive negative action. That is, when you tell yourself, "I don't want to go there," you are saying this is a place to avoid and you highlight this area to your brain. You are emphasizing a negative target and are probably unaware that you are giving this avoidance command a great deal of focused energy and attention. Your brain recognizes the signal as a spurt of energy that demands focus. By trying to put it out of your mind and suppressing the thought or image, you are actually bringing it to life.

DON'T TOUCH! THE IRONIC PROCESS THEORY IN ACTION

For example, a child is in the kitchen and watching his mother cooking something and becomes curious about the orange glow of the electric oven, so he asks what is happening. His mother replies that she is cooking and for the child to get his hands away from the stove. His mother commands him, while he's curious, "Don't touch the stove!" So, what happens? The child wants to find out for himself and touches the stove. The child burns himself and his mother screams, *"What did I just tell you not to do!"* She adds, "I told you not to touch the stove, didn't I? But you had to find out for yourself, didn't you! I said, 'Don't touch the stove'!" Every one of us has probably been that little kid who touched the stove and learned the hard way through trial and error.

Although we went through a lot of Band-Aids and first-aid cream, we had to find out for ourselves. The word *don't* did not stop us, but rather, it was a signal to proceed and do exactly the opposite. This is the ironic thought process in action. That is, if you direct yourself to not do something, you are likely to end up with the result you are trying to avoid. The brain doesn't understand the word *don't* as much as it responds to the energy that you are directing to the object or action you are trying to avoid.

The ironic process theory suggests that the more you try to suppress a thought and gain mental control over a thing, the more the mind works to insure that very thing comes to the surface even stronger. That is the irony. What you didn't want to have happen you create by trying to compel it away with mental control. In golf, when you say to yourself, "Don't go to the right!," what does your mind tell your body? It suggests that there is energy to the right, and the last word in your command becomes the object of your attention and focus. Your intention was to not go right, and when you swing and the ball goes to the right, you say to yourself, "That is exactly what I didn't want to happen!" By giving yourself a *don't* command, you are almost insuring that what you don't want to happen . . . will happen.

So what do you do? Here is the key. You always give yourself a *do this* perspective. Instead of saying commands from a negative, reframe your focus and tell yourself that this is what you want to *do*. The *do this* perspective is vital to golfing success!

NIKE AND "JUST DO IT"

A great example of a *do* mentality is the brand Nike. Nike has $16 billion in revenue per year with sales all over the globe. The slogan that they adopted years ago represents their action code: "Just Do It." The Nike swoosh has come to represent positive and purposeful action. It silently suggests that a person who wears Nike clothes and shoes can achieve the possible. That is the by-product of their product line. Nike is in the possibility business. But what if Nike's trademark swoosh had a question mark in the center? Would their slogan change from "Just Do It" to "Boy, I Hope This Works"? That is the type of commitment (or lack of) that most people step into the ball with and hope to have some success. Instead of stepping in and hitting the ball with purposeful intent, most golfers bail out on their commitment and adopt a strategy of "hit and hope." This noncommittal rarely achieves success on the golf course. Choose to go after your goals with a *do* mentality. If it worked for Phil Knight and company, I am sure that it can work for you as well.

For you to move into possibility thinking, the following section will give you effective strategies to quiet your mind and direct your focus to purposeful action.

DR. BOB'S Rx FOR ELIMINATING AN OVERACTIVE MIND

1. **Think . . . then act!** You must have a well-conceived plan for each shot *before* you step into the ball. Most golfers are ill prepared when they step into the ball with no clue about what they are going to do with the shot. They become rattled and have a dozen swing thoughts in their head, which leads to tension and doubt. Most golfers hit the ball without any plan at all! I love what legendary basketball coach John Wooden once stated about planning: "If you fail to plan, you are just planning

to fail." This is golfing gospel. You absolutely must know what you want to do with the shot before you step in to hit it!

To remedy the miscue of stepping into the ball without a plan, you need to focus and make a decision *behind the ball*. Make a firm decision about the type of shot you will hit and what club it will take. When you have made this decision, only then should you step in and address your ball. Keep your thought simple and specific. *Have a single, yet simple, swing thought and a specific target. This will help quiet intruding random thoughts.*

2. **Commit to a specific plan.** After having decided what type of shot you want to hit, commit to your decision. Committing to your shot plan is a promise that you will make a purposeful action. By honoring your commitment, you are saying, "I will do this thing now!" Committing to your shot, to the feel of the golf swing, and to your target are all parts of honoring your commitment. Commitment means that your single focus is on this shot and that nothing else will distract you from carrying it out.

3. **You *will* have random thoughts.** No matter how strong your mental focus, a random thought or two may enter your consciousness. It is important to realize and accept that you are human. Being human you have a constant stream of thoughts entering your mind. A thought can pop into your consciousness from anywhere. So, whenever you are stepping into your shot, recognize that you may have a stray thought or two. Your task is to step into the ball and have a single, specific focus. If you

find yourself being distracted by a random thought, allow it to pass and gently remind yourself to "stay on target." Allow the thought to pass; do not try to force it out. Do not feel that you have to suppress what you do not want. Trying to force your concentration away from something is a sure bet that you will bring it more into your awareness. Dismissing or not paying attention to a random or negative thought allows it to dry up and blow away. If you find that the thought is too distracting, simply step back, refocus, recommit to your decision, and start fresh.

4. **Keep things simple.** As Robert Damron suggested, keeping things simple without too many mechanical thoughts is perhaps the best way to play. Many golfers when they play their best golf say they are not thinking about anything at all! In reality, their focus is on the target and not on themselves. Therefore, keep a single swing focus or swing cue that will aid you to focus on swinging to your target. A simple word cue such as *smooth* or *oily* works wonders for giving you a body sense of smooth motion and rhythm. It doesn't make much sense to have more than one swing key because the brain cannot handle the information overload. You do not want to create helmet fire in your head! I love the acronym KISS. It means "keep it simple and specific." The next time you play, limit your self-talk and self-instruction. Keep your swing thought to a single word, thought, or image. The golf swing is one area where less is more!

5. **Just Do It.** The slogan that has become part of Nike's image is a reminder that you have a plan and your job

now is to carry it out. As you are addressing the ball, remind yourself that your task is to swing to your target. Give yourself the *do* command rather than the avoidance command of *don't*. Remember that your brain doesn't understand the negative connotation of the word *don't*, but it does recognize the energy that you bring to it. So, instead of saying "Don't leave this putt short," rephrase it to "I do want to roll my ball into the right center of the cup!" Giving yourself a *do* direction rather than a *don't* provides you with a positive focus for purposeful action, rather than for an action to avoid failure.

TAKE IT TO THE COURSE!

1. Ninety-nine percent of all golf success comes from being ready for action. Make sure that you have a clear plan for your shot before you step into the address position. Adhering to your well-rehearsed routine will keep you in the present moment.
2. Behind the ball, visualize the entire picture and view it with a positive and accurate focus. Negative visualization about where the shot might go is not the way to think. Focus your mind on what you want to happen . . . not on what you want to avoid!
3. Just like the Nike image . . . get yourself into a "Just Do It" mind-set. Decide what you want to do and give yourself permission to do it.

(continued)

4. Get your mind into a "yes" mind-set and focus.
5. Remember that your mind will have random thoughts. Allow the random thoughts and chaos to clear before you swing. If your focus is distracted . . . pause for a second and get your eyes back to where you want the ball to go, which will gently bring you back into proper focus.

NINE

I Lose My Composure

*Failure is good. It's fertilizer. Everything I've learned
about coaching, I've learned from making mistakes.*
—RICK PITINO

MIND-SETS AND MOOD-SETS

Keeping your composure on the golf course is not as easy as it
sounds. Now, when your shots are going straight to the target
and your putts are dropping, it's easy to be calm and composed
and full of confidence. But what happens to your emotional
outlook when the putts don't drop or your shots go all over the
place? How easy is it to be calm and confident then?

Or what happens to your game strategy when you are having your best day ever and you become so excited that you start
to worry that you will not finish well and will mess up your
score? You start to doubt your ability because you are playing
almost too well! This is akin to the notion that one can't stand
prosperity or too much good fortune. Why does this happen?

By its nature, golf is a tough game filled with emotional

highs and lows. Not only is it a thinking game filled with strategy and precision, but it also has a huge physical component that borders on requiring perfection. This quest for ultimate golf efficiency creates many stressful situations. How you deal with and accept these minitasks and execute to the best of your ability creates a lot of mental and emotional strain. The great Jack Nicklaus said that composure helped him win more tournaments than any other factor. In reflecting back on his storied career, Jack said he could only remember one time when he lost his emotional balance. This is a testament to the strength of his mental skill. It is easy to get lost in the ups and downs of golf. One needs to be ready for anything that may happen along the journey down the fairways.

For example, you can be going along with a full head of steam and playing with total confidence, then hit a shot straight out of bounds and damage your score and your psyche. How do you recover from something totally unexpected? Where do you get rid of your frustration? How do you get over your disappointment that your results don't match your expectations? Is it possible to vent or have an emotional catharsis and still create positive momentum and confidence?

These are all questions that every golfer faces in almost every round. The noticeable difference between good players and poor ones is the ability of the good players to stay emotionally balanced and mentally engaged with every shot. Golf is unlike team sports in that wherever your mind and mood go, you have no one to applaud or blame but yourself. You are either the champion or the chump. But unlike dynamic sports such as football, basketball, or soccer, where you can run off your frustration or have an emotional catharsis by hitting a ball or playing more aggressively on defense, golf does not give you much of a chance to blow off steam. The controlled aggression within the sport of golf demands a tighter focus and a stronger rein on one's moods and behaviors.

This leads to the inevitable question of which is more important, mind-set or mood-set? If we talk about the mind being what the brain does and controlling the actions of the body, where does the emotional affect of one's mood fit in? If the mind is in control, then why do a golfer's strong feelings, that rush of emotions, overwhelm his or her logic and decision making? These are difficult questions for even neuropsychologists to answer, but one thing is certain: golf is a multifaceted and multidimensional sport that demands control of not only one's thoughts, but also of one's emotions and behaviors.

The brain and limbic system in coordination with the autonomic nervous system create a powerful athletic organism capable of extraordinary performance. But when one is a bit off or out of sync, it definitely affects the other. Balance between a great mind and a productive mood is paramount for optimum performance. However, having mental and emotional balance isn't just about being emotionally neutral or not feeling anything at all, as is the case for an automaton or robot. Being emotionally balanced is about staying in control and having your wits about you when things go either poorly or even well. Sometimes, things go almost too well! You can be affected by being too "up" as much as you can be affected by being too "down." Let me explain this a bit further.

EXCITEMENT AND MAJOR CHAMPIONSHIPS

Losing one's composure when one is enraged or frustrated is common in golf. The examples of how bad bounces and poor results can change a player's attitude are almost too numerous to list here. But composure can also be lost by having success. Although not as common, it happens, and the fallout is sometimes just as devastating. A prime example of someone who suffered not from anger but from overwhelming elation is World Golf Hall of Fame member and multiple Major Championship winner Larry Nelson. Larry describes his mental mistake as being a combination of psychological and physiological factors and his inability to calm himself during a hormonal rush. Excitement from his great play carried over into the next few holes and cost him some valuable shots, perhaps even a Major Championship.

My greatest mental mistake wasn't just a mental one, but it was a physiological one as well. I don't mean a physical mistake of the swing, but one where I just couldn't get my body to quiet itself because of the adrenaline rush that was created. It happened when I made a huge putt in the '83 US Open on hole number sixteen. I became so excited that I couldn't calm myself down to hit successive successful shots into the following hole. On seventeen I chunked a tee shot short and had to hit a seven iron where I would normally have hit a sand iron or wedge.

I did the same thing again in the '84 Masters. After I had just sunk a big putt on hole number eleven and went to hole number twelve, I hit my tee ball fat. My mental mistake was that I just couldn't calm myself enough to hit the shot that I needed to hit. I think that time was the enemy here. I just didn't have enough time to let the adrenaline rush dissolve. It was difficult to maintain my composure.

To his credit, Larry went on to win the 1983 US Open by one shot over the defending champion, Tom Watson. Not only that, but Larry overcame his brief loss of composure to fire a final-round 67 amid the Open's grueling physical and psychological test, held that year at Oakmont Country Club. We can learn from Larry that having mental and emotional balance isn't just about recovering from bad shots and poor results, but maintaining composure as well when great things are happening.

Larry said that during the '83 US Open, after making a great putt on hole sixteen, he couldn't calm himself down in order to hit an effective tee shot on seventeen. The rush following his putt skyrocketed his adrenal system, and Larry had to counter the effects of a metabolic spike to his system. He missed his tee ball on seventeen and had to hit much more club on his approach than he would normally have played. When things are going well, the human body can become so revved up that it is hard to create a balanced playing focus. Remaining in the moment and not becoming too high or too low is vital for optimal performance. Time becomes crucial as the body needs a sufficient period to absorb the influx of hormones and create a balanced state. Even with the breathing techniques that Larry applied walking from the sixteenth green to the seventeenth tee, he found it hard to counter the effects of his elation. To his credit, he managed sufficient focus to close the round with solid play and win his second Major Championship.

Conversely, from Larry's statement we can also learn that extreme joy, or eustress, which is the opposite of distress or stress, can cause playing problems from which we fail to recover. During the final round at the 1984 Masters, Larry came into Amen Corner having just holed a birdie putt on the tough eleventh hole. Feeling buoyant, Larry took the brief stroll to the twelfth tee at Augusta National. With the thousands that throng the ropes and surround the tee box, it is an emotional challenge to not get caught up in all the excitement. Larry was in the hunt for another Major Championship, and now he was facing the most demanding hole in Major Championship golf . . . number twelve at Augusta!

Twelve is so demanding because the green angles away from the player on the tee box, and precarious winds swirl around Amen Corner. Making a clear and focused decision on the tee shot at twelve is fundamental to success. Having just made a birdie on eleven and hearing the enthusiastic applause from the crowd surrounding the tee on twelve made it difficult for Larry to calm himself. He hit his shot fat and ended up with a final round of 70, which was good for fifth place.

Larry says that in both of these major tournaments, elation caused an imbalance in his mind and mood. Larry's excitement altered his feelings of strength, touch, and coordinated movement. It also affected his thoughts. Think about your own game: How many times have you had a series of birdies or great scoring opportunities and you became too excited? You probably started getting ahead of yourself and became overconfident in your decision making and shot strategy.

Although a feeling of strong positive momentum is good, a balanced and grounded approach is needed. Staying focused when good things are happening is a challenge, but it is a nicer challenge than that when things head in the opposite direction. Poor results often create rage and disappointment, which interfere with our golfing enjoyment and occur more frequently than we would like. Let's take a closer look at the dark side of mental and emotional imbalance.

WHO AM I? DR. JEKYLL OR MR. HYDE?

You are playing with your buddies and having a great day when suddenly your best friend erupts into a rage because he has just hit his ball into the water. Without much fanfare and with little time to accept his result or allow his disappointment to simmer down, he throws down another ball and promptly sends another white orb to swim with the fishes. You observe your friend and happy golfer now becoming a maniacal and ugly character. A metamorphosis has taken place in only a few seconds. Why does this happen? Why do golfers become so emotional when their results go awry, and why do players who seem relatively under control lose control so easily?

When players' results do not match their expectations, they can become angry, resentful, depressed, and downright ugly. They turn from an optimistic and hopeful golfer into a sour and pessimistic player. This is known in the psychological world as an emotional hijacking. Without players' being aware of the rapid change in their feelings, their thoughts and attitudes are suddenly turned in the opposite direction and create a runaway train that is earmarked for disaster. Not meeting one's expectations creates an anger that one has failed to play to one's talent level. Instead of accepting the result and allowing the poor shot sequence to pass, golfers immediately fill their mind with distorted thoughts and feelings. They ruminate about their misfortune and start to berate themselves internally and many times emote with voiced outbursts and profanity. An emotional kidnapping has taken place, and the perpetrator is our own mind! This transformation is similar to that in Robert Louis

Stevenson's *The Strange Case of Dr. Jekyll and Mr. Hyde.* This story illustrates the duality of good versus evil and the notion of having a split or altered personality. Many golfers who play regularly and with great intensity tend toward this duality. They take their golf so seriously and so often get caught up in their golfing furor that they tend to resemble the acidic Mr. Hyde much more often than the good-natured Dr. Jekyll. This emotional yo-yo occurs even in the best of players. The emotional highs and lows are similar to being on a roller coaster with nowhere to go but round and round and up and down until the ride is over and then you throw up! Who needs this type of distraction when you are attempting to be on an even keel for maximum precision and accuracy? The key is to be aware of when you are out of control and to find your optimal emotional state for performing.

CHANNELING THE INTENSITY

When discussing emotional composure, remember that passion is an important attribute in one's mental and emotional profile. Passion adds a spark to someone's talent, and it is important to fuel the passion but not let the intensity get out of control. It is much like cooking a steak on a grill. The flame must be at a point where it sears the meat, but if the grill becomes too hot, you scorch and burn it. In golf, you want to have the fire burning deep from within but to a controlled point. Too little heat and you are uninspired and play lethargically; too much heat and you flame out of control. It's important to be aware of your emotional state so that your intensity is channeled to deliver the proper amount of motivation and focus to play at your optimum level.

Someone who plays golf with a lot of passion is Drew Weaver, of High Point, North Carolina. Drew is a young professional whom I have worked with for many years, and when we first met, his fiery temper and emotional outbursts showed up in his junior golf tournaments. He was beating himself up because he was trying too hard and playing with too much emotion. Blessed with enormous eye-hand coordination and a deep competitive spirit, Drew tended to get in his own way by being unaware of how his emotions changed his playing style and course management. He wanted so badly to make things happen that he would sabotage his balanced emotional state and become frustrated and discouraged.

When Drew finally learned how to channel his intensity and anger into positive energy, it helped him to become the first American in over twenty-nine years to win the British Amateur, in 2007, and also to become a member of the winning 2009 United States Walker Cup team. Drew is now a touring professional whose strong emotional fire and mental discipline have led him to much success. Here he talks about his greatest mental mistake:

I think my biggest mental mistake is that I become too emotional and my mood tends to turn sour. I become discouraged and angry when the results don't happen or when I have been playing well and I have bad breaks. My emotions tend to get the best of me, and I then start to press and force things to happen, and that creates more poor shots and increases the negative spiral downward.

I just don't know why I get so angry about things, but I

(continued)

tend to be an emotional player and I play with a lot of heart. I think the main issue is that I get too up when I hit good shots, and I tend to get too down when I hit bad shots. It just isn't all that balanced. When I let my emotions get the best of me, what I have to do is take a mental time-out and let the dust settle. I take a mental time-out and just take a couple of deep breaths and try and put the past behind me. I like to start fresh and with a new outlook on the next shot. But, if I let the bad shots linger, it becomes very tough to turn it around.

But I have to put things in perspective and start over. It isn't easy, but it can be done. When I have emotional composure and play with an even-keel mind frame, I tend to play my best golf. Nothing seems to bother me, but when I become a bit too emotional, the wheels start to wobble and hopefully I can right the ship before they fall off.

What stands out the most from Drew's statements is his awareness of his emotional state. He acknowledges that he is a feel player, but is unsure why he becomes so angry. He has now learned to manage more effectively his being an emotional player and playing with a lot of heart. During his career and our work together, he has incorporated specific psychological techniques that allow him to cool down and move into a more productive mental and emotional state. Drew knows when he becomes too up from hitting a good shot or too down from hitting a poor shot. This is known as monitoring your arousal level. When you realize you are becoming too highly aroused, you try to bring your activation level down a notch or two. When you are feeling a bit blah or apathetic over a shot, then you need to motivate yourself and pump yourself up to a higher arousal.

The key element to Drew's success is his knowledge that when his emotions take over, he needs to step back and refocus his attention into something more positive and productive. Drew has learned to "start fresh" with a new perspective for the upcoming shot. This single idea helps to readjust his mental and emotional thermostat. An even temperament helps him to play his best golf—to the extent that nothing tends to bother him. As he states, it isn't easy to do, but it can be done. The same can be true for you as well!

TEMPERAMENT AND EMOTIONAL BALANCE

Another golfer who spoke of the even temperament was Hall of Fame golfer Bob Charles. Bob was addressing key aspects of Bobby Locke and Peter Thomson, two all-time greats, who never changed their outer demeanor or temperament while they were playing. For Bob Charles, this observation was vital to his development as a professional golfer.

Mentally, I think Peter Thomson and Bobby Locke were the best I have seen because they had very consistent emotional temperaments. Their demeanors about how they went about their business on the course were so focused and stable. I happen to think that the players of today are way too emotional and have too many large mood swings.

I remember one time when Bobby Locke played Sam Snead sixteen different times and defeated him fourteen of those

(*continued*)

sixteen times. The thing about Locke was that even when he was in the lead with Sam or way behind, I never saw him have a different pace in his step or his routine. He was always the same. His temperament never changed. That was a truly amazing thing to observe how focused and emotionally stable he was.

We learn from Bob Charles that Peter Thomson and Bobby Locke had the ability to maintain their stable mental and emotional state regardless of how well or poorly they were performing. Bob suggests that the players of today are too emotional and have too large mood swings. Perhaps this observation reflects that back in the days when Bobby Locke, Sam Snead, and Peter Thomson were playing, match play was more in vogue than it is today. If in head-to-head match play an opponent saw that you were losing composure and starting to despair, it would give him an advantage mentally. Therefore, a stoic demeanor would hide that you might have been crumbling inside.

Bob says that Bobby Locke in his matches with Sam Snead always had the same tempo and rhythm in his routine, no matter if Locke was ahead or behind. Consistency in his preshot routine perhaps helped him to stay emotionally stable and outwardly composed. Thus, you could say that consistency of mind and mood helps in consistency of shot execution. That would certainly hold true for Bobby Locke, Sam Snead, and Peter Thomson.

However, in contrast to players such as Thomson and Locke, many golfers of today show their frustration and have volatile outbursts. Quite a few players over the past several years have been demonstrative and worn their emotions on their sleeves, including such storied names as Seve Ballesteros, Steve Pate, Pat

Perez, Craig Stadler, Woody Austin, and most notably Tiger Woods. But, we may want to ask ourselves, is showing our emotions such a bad thing? If the world's number one player emotes and has a brief tantrum now and then, how can that be perceived as something that may be hurtful to our performance? I think the answer may lie with touring professional Scott Walsh of Palo Alto, California.

> My greatest mistake is that I just get a bit out of control and I can't think straight after a bad shot. I think that my emotions just take over and I am not at the same emotional level as when I started my round. I just let my emotions take over after a bad shot or a shot that I wasn't expecting, and I just don't really get over it. The bad thing is that I fail to learn anything from it after I have hit it.
>
> I just get angry and frustrated and take that anger into the next shot. The emotion clouds my judgment and thinking and I never get to the root of the problem. I want to be more honest with myself on why I am playing poorly instead of just reacting poorly to the shot and the situation that I find myself in.

HOLDING YOURSELF HOSTAGE

Scott Walsh's greatest mistake is one made by many other golfers. Many golfers never fully recover after a bad shot or a bad hole. They simply take their "garbage" from that situation and carry it to the next shot, and the cycle repeats until the round is damaged beyond repair. The sad part of this story is that the emotional kidnapping takes place without the conscious awareness of the player. You have held yourself hostage by your lack of acceptance and your frustration. Lack of acceptance of a poor result that turns into anger is an emotional crime. The penalty for this is higher scores and loss of confidence. Touring professional Brian Davis states that nothing good can come from losing your composure when things turn bad during a round of golf:

> I think my greatest mistake during my career is that I haven't let go of a bad shot and I carried it to the next shot or hole. I know that everyone can say that they have to accept the results that you create, but it is much easier to say than it is to do. Everyone needs to do a better job of accepting, and the sooner you realize that for yourself, the better off you will be.
>
> I mean, there is nothing good that is going to come out of being negative. It can only hurt you, and if you don't release the past and move on, your day will be over quickly. The tough part is that you have to really try to learn how to accept, and the better you can do that and create emotional balance is when you really start to see some improvement in your game and into your shots that you are hitting.

Think about the many times that you have played and let a round be spoiled by being disappointed and angry. After the round was over, you probably thought to yourself, Where did it all go wrong? Why didn't I just do this or that? The reason is, you were not thinking clearly or logically. Instead, your emotions were running the show, and you reacted (poorly) rather than taking the time to let things settle and then making a decision. As the saying goes, "haste makes waste," and many players throw strokes away in the haste of their frustration rather than taking the time to let the dust settle and to make clear and well-thought-out decisions.

What is particularly important in both Scott's and Brian's revelations is that their emotions are not on the same level as when they started their rounds. This indicates they have been negatively affected by their score or results. Scott talks of how he becomes overly emotional after a poor or unexpected shot. This is where the sabotage of one's composure and confidence begins. When your result does not match your expectations, you become disappointed, discouraged, and many times enraged.

DEALING WITH DISAPPOINTMENT . . . POORLY

Many golfers take out their frustration on their clubs, the course, their playing companions, their golf bag, and many times themselves with profane and demoralizing statements. With this negative self-talk and verbal abuse, golfers damage their psyche and golf esteem and destroy momentum or confidence. Once such statements as "You're terrible, you're pathetic . . . get out of the game!" become lodged in your mind, the emotional fallout sometimes makes it hard to put the pieces back together. The negative feelings and thoughts cause us to go into a downward spiral. Not only is your psyche affected, but the massive doses of stress hormones such as cortisol and epinephrine that have entered your bloodstream take hours for your body to eliminate. The old saying "Sticks and stones may break my bones but words will never hurt me!" is absolutely false. Negative and demeaning words create further anger, neurosis, feelings of inferiority, and resentment and create emotional scars that take a long time to heal. Treating the wound with soothing words is first aid for the disappointed.

Scott's and Brian's statements teach us that it is easier to get angry at yourself and become negative than it is to accept your result and move on with renewed enthusiasm and optimism. The sooner you learn to compose yourself and realize that getting angry doesn't help you, the sooner your results will become better.

Scott says his anger clouds his judgment. This affects his ability to think clearly about his dilemma and to make the appropriate adjustments so that he can move on to the next shot. He talks about not learning anything and not getting to the root of the problem. This issue escalates and then the real damage is done. He can't remedy the situation and it carries over into the next series of shots.

This loss of emotional control and composure happens to millions of golfers around the globe. They fail to execute properly or make a single mistake, then become angry and allow the negative thoughts and feelings to fester. Their anger gains strength and they fuel the fire and create more mistakes, and it continues until they have damaged the complete round. Many golfers need at least two or three holes to regain emotional composure after a bad shot, and in that brief period much scoring damage, let alone the mental scarring, is done.

ROLE MODEL FOR BAD BEHAVIOR?

If we use a few professionals as models and especially those that emote and sometimes explode, we need to remember one thing:

they are professionals. These select few (and I do mean few . . . *roughly one-tenth of 1 percent of the total golf population*) have made golf their vocation. They play the game for money and they will hit hundreds of thousands of shots in their career. They have also trained themselves to eradicate any carryover from a bad shot and move on mentally unscathed to the next shot. The few professionals who outwardly wear their emotions on their sleeves have trained themselves to make a living out of playing golf. Yes, they have much intensity and passion, and their frustration does come out. They are human and have their moments of weakness the same as the rest of us. But are they proper role models for the rest of the golfing world? I do not think so. The consequences for emotional outbursts and unregulated passion may be too high a price to pay for the recreational or amateur player. Keeping things in the proper perspective and emotional balance provides a greater foundation for consistent play.

Even the elite have interventions or specific strategies that help them eliminate the frustration and stabilize their emotions from a poor shot or event and clear their minds before they move into the next shot. If they fail to do this, they are not professionals for long. Or, at least not the ones who make money. The whims of their emotional turmoil will cause them to break down as well. Why is that? Simple: they are human beings, and as human beings we tend to let ourselves and others down. We are all the products of the type of emotional fuel that we give ourselves through our self-directed thoughts and feelings. If we give ourselves positive fuel in the form of great thoughts and feelings, we can perform to unbelievable heights. Place contaminated fuel or negative thoughts in our brain and we will eventually break down. The brain will only carry out the commands that you give it. Choose wisely.

One final thing needs to be mentioned when discussing those players who curse, throw clubs, and show negative emotions on the golf course. We may never know, but one wonders how good these volatile players might have become if they had channeled their negative energy into something a bit more effective. They might even have won more tournaments and been more effective than they have been. I have yet to hear of an elite golfer attribute his success to his abusive and angry behavior. For the rest of the golfing population, maintaining their composure and letting go of frustration and anger is perhaps one of the most important things they can do to let their true talent come out.

The following section provides some proven intervention techniques for dealing with emotional frustration on the golf course. Diligence with these strategies is vital for success. Overcoming tendencies to anger and frustration is a difficult chore for any golfer, and it does take time. Learning how to deal with your emotions, both good and bad, and to channel your energy in a more productive manner will help you to maintain composure and increase your chances of success on the links.

DR. BOB'S Rx FOR REGAINING COMPOSURE

1. **First things first! Recognize when you are becoming frustrated.** Awareness is key. The biggest part of the battle for your mind and mood is to catch yourself when you first start to become irritated, touchy, or generally discouraged. Catch yourself early and tell yourself that you are too smart a player to let your emotions dictate

how you react to this situation. While you are playing and *starting* to feel discouraged, ask yourself, *Am I in control of my golf game? Or is my golf game in control of me?* Then, count from one to five and take a deep breath. After exhaling, tell yourself that you can handle this situation and that you will let this minor irritation pass. Take another deep breath and then move on to your next shot. Having done this, you will be in a better place.

2. **The three-step swing-away.** Do *not* take your anger into your next shot after you have just hit a poor shot! Many golfers hit a poor shot and instantly react angrily and immediately start to walk toward their next shot or head to the golf cart. They carry their anger with them and either throw their club in the bag or walk hastily to their next shot so that they can ruin that one as well. They are taking their emotional trash from one shot to another. Do not be a garbageman! Do not allow yourself to place your golf club in your bag without doing this swing-away drill. Instead of being angry, try this simple, three-step system to clear your mind and regain composure.

Step one. After watching your result, instead of tossing the club in the bag, take two aggressive, controlled swings and swing away the frustration and anger. Allow yourself this opportunity to vent.

Step two. After completing the two dynamic swing-aways, take a third and final swing. However, make this a real-time swing that reflects what you wanted to do with the original shot. Rehearse the swing and create a good feeling that you want to remember. By doing this you are putting on via a positive stroke a good feeling for the club you just hit poorly. Thus the next time you reach for that same club, you are not reaching for a mistake but a positive feeling that will promote success for the upcoming shot!

Step three. Place the club back in the bag and take a deep breath and move on. Placing the club in the bag and not slamming it provides closure for this shot. Taking a deep breath and moving on signals a fresh start to the upcoming shot, which you can approach feeling composed and confident for whatever lies ahead.

3. **The ten-step walk-away procedure.** This intervention compartmentalizes one's emotional state using a specific behavior and a time element to settle oneself down. The system has worked well for Tiger Woods and may work well for you. Tiger is known for his passion and intense fury on the golf course, and much to his credit he can move from one shot into the next without carrying the baggage of poor results or frustrated performance. Tiger uses ten steps and a time element to dismiss the past so that he can move forward fresh and ready for whatever lies ahead. He uses a distance of ten yards as a boundary line to eliminate his frustration from one shot to the next. If he hits his shot and becomes frustrated, he has set a limit of ten steps in which to clear his mind and move from the old into the new. As he walks from his last shot and strides toward his next, he has trained his mind and emotions to leave any emotional baggage behind. By the time he takes his tenth step, the last shot is history. It is gone. He has placed that shot behind him, parked the frustration, and is now walking forward leaving the past in the shadows. You can use ten steps or how many you need for this procedure to work for you. By giving

yourself a dismissal boundary line, you are proclaiming that by the time you reach the boundary, your mind is clear and your emotions are being channeled into the next shot, and that the past poor results are just that . . . the past.

4. **The rubber-band snap.** This intervention calls upon both cognitive and behavioral aspects to be active participants in regaining focus and composure. You will need a good-size rubber band. Place it on either wrist, preferably your left if you are right-handed, vice versa if you are left-handed. The rubber band is a tool to remind you that whenever you feel frustrated or overly excited or are using profanity or acting poorly, you should tell yourself to *stop!* When you tell yourself to stop, grab your rubber band and pull it back a good ways and let it snap into your wrist. Immediately after you do this, tell yourself that you do not want to feel like this, and remind yourself of something that you *can do* and *will do* in the upcoming shot. This can be an uplifting word or cue or even reminding yourself that you have done this before. The important thing is that you are stopping the poor thoughts and behavior and you are gaining control and redirecting your focus into something more positive. I have players for whom this technique has worked wonders, not only for their emotional stability, but in keeping them focused and not drifting into the future or projecting about their score. The first few days that you do this, you may be surprised at how many times you need to give yourself a good snap. It may also surprise you how fast you learn to recognize your mistakes and not repeat the poor thought patterns that have plagued you in the past.

5. **Change your self-talk.** How we talk to ourselves is a great indicator of our self-concept and how we honor (or dishonor) ourselves. If you berate yourself with negative comments or are simply disgusted, take the time to tell yourself it's time to change. Assess how you are feeling and monitor the thoughts and emotions that are spewing forth. Changing the way you talk to yourself will change the way you feel. Use words that are cooler in tone and do not have such a "hot reactor" quality to them and you will be surprised at how calm your overall temperament becomes. For example, instead of saying "That shot is terrible!" replace it with "That shot is ineffective." If you feel your swing is not working, instead of saying "I just don't have it today—I am done!" replace it with "I am due to hit a good one sooner or later . . . let's stay committed to the process." The sooner you can change your language, the sooner you will feel its effect with your body. When you use negative words, you stir up stress hormones such as cortisol and epinephrine. By using words that are more soothing, you release other hormones, such as oxytocin, dopamine, and serotonin, that promote stabilization of the nervous system and calm the body. Change your self-talk and your behaviors change as well.

6. **Maintain a consistent tempo and rhythm with your routine.** Becoming angry, excited, and frustrated clouds your judgment and disrupts your natural body rhythm. Your body is already aroused, and when arousal is too high, it affects your performance. It also affects your ability to perform automatically. As was discussed earlier, like great players such as Peter Thomson and Bobby Locke you will

want to make your routine as consistent and rhythmic as possible. The structure of your preshot and preputt routines should provide a consistent pace for all of your subsequent behaviors. When golfers become mad, excited, anxious, or frustrated, they generally speed up their routine or sometimes even abandon their routine totally! Take the time to go through your routine thoroughly, and monitor your tempo as you are getting ready to hit. Slowing yourself down and keeping things on an even keel are simple yet effective ways to keep the swing flowing.

7. **Remember the basics. Start with *one* shot**. It is so easy to become angry when you are scoring high numbers and you feel you are wasting shots. Instead of thinking about numbers, outcome, how many shots you have given away, or what your final score might be, focus on the most important number in golf: *one*. Get your mind back into playing one shot at a time and create a minisuccess pattern. Just as we create positive momentum one shot at a time and start to get on a roll, we also need to stop the bogey and double-bogey bleeding and apply a mental tourniquet. Get yourself back to the basic idea of doing the best you can with the shot you are about to hit. You need to start fresh on this single shot. This is the only shot that you can control now. Park your frustration and your anger and make a concerted effort to hit this shot as well as you can. Remind yourself to adhere to a good rhythm and put your mind on your target. You will be surprised at how a bit of redirected focus can turn your day around. But you must start with the present shot, the shot of *one*.

8. **Parking your anger.** Parking your anger is a cognitive-behavioral technique that means that once a shot is done, you put it behind you and move on. *Parking* means to leave your frustrations and unmet expectations behind and to walk away from that spot. For example, if you have a used tissue in your hand, do you carry it around with you? Not likely. You find the nearest trash container and dispose of it. This is the basic concept of parking your anger. Once you have finished with a shot, accept it for what it is and move on. The important point to realize in the acceptance phase is that once a shot is hit, you can do nothing more with it. It is history, a done deal. Your task now is to accept it for what it is, good or bad, and to move on. If you are disappointed or discouraged, you need to park this feeling and leave it behind. Many times players take a deep breath, place the club in their bag, and readjust their glove or hat . . . and then walk, but never before they have done those behaviors. Parking your anger means to give yourself a moment to let the dust settle, then to walk away and leave your golfing garbage behind.

TAKE IT TO THE COURSE!

1. Remain cool, calm, and collected. Emotional balance is vital! Golf is a game of many highs and lows. The key is to stay emotionally stable and balanced. Do not become overly excited when things are going well. Do not

(continued)

get too down when things aren't going well. Staying emotionally balanced allows you to play with the best mind-set and mood-set for optimum golf.

2. If you hit a poor shot . . . do not become upset and instantly react. Pause . . . take a couple of deep breaths. Before you react, take a second or two to recover, then swing away your frustration and anger. Taking two swing-away motions allows you to reset your mental compass and allow the bad feelings to pass.

3. Before you put your club into the bag, make sure that you have created a good feeling with a rehearsal swing of what you wanted to make in the first place. By doing this, you are putting a good feeling into your bag and not allowing anger to become a passenger for the next shot.

4. Patience is confidence waiting to happen! Stay composed and realize that good things will come if you hang in there and persevere with a balanced mood-set.

5. Give yourself a pep talk after things go awry. Allowing negative thoughts to manifest into destructive feelings can make your round take a serious turn for the worse. Keep yourself moving in a positive direction with a verbal boost.

Epilogue

As you have discovered, no one is immune to the capricious and invisible forces of a faulty mind-set. What you have just read is a small part of the cornucopia of mental calamities that beset us all. Whether you are a Hall of Fame golfer or a struggling amateur, all of us suffer from these cognitive aberrations. Just like the many players who have been kind enough to open up their thoughts and feelings to discuss their mental calamities, you, too, will have a number of mental demons waiting to be exorcised.

I am extremely grateful to all of the contributors that helped make this book so interesting to write. I am also indebted to the prepublication readers who examined my manuscript only to find themselves immersed in descriptions for their own lack of golfing success. In particular, after one of my golf instructors at my Nike Junior Golf School at Williams College in Williamstown, Massachusetts, read the raw manuscript, she started to cry. I asked her what was wrong and she replied, "Every one of these issues is describing me!" While reading, she saw in black and white a revelation of what she had been doing and feeling for the past five years. She said, "If I had this information five years ago . . . it would have made a huge difference in my amateur and college career." My reply was that there is no going back, but to take this information and create something wonderful with it from this point forward. The same can be true for you. Her mistake is a common one, illustrated in this book again and again. That is, we make the mental mistake, and we fail to learn from it and move forward. We simply react to the calamity and relive the agony again and again until it becomes a dominant negative mental habit.

This book was written for the treatment of these afflictions and to help golfers move forward and prevent further emotional pain on the links. After all, the game was designed to be a recreational pursuit filled with joyous highs and lows, not to be an endeavor of frustration and work!

What is featured within this book is only a small portion of the many items that plague golfers. I have researched a host of others, and they will be explored in another volume, to be titled *The Back Nine*. If you like what is written here or would like to find out how to enhance your mental game, I invite you to visit my website, www.drbobwinters.com, or to contact me personally at drbob@drbobwinters.com, as listed in the contact section of my Web site. Individuals, groups, and corporations are always welcome, and I would love to hear from you! Remember, help for your golf game is only a touch of your hand away from my eyes and ears. I hope you have enjoyed the information herein and play mistake-free golf!

May you always play without mistakes,

Dr. Robert K. Winters
Sport Psychologist, Orlando, Florida

ACKNOWLEDGMENTS

It goes without saying that getting a book from the conception of an author's thought into the hands of an interested reader is no easy task. The years of labor and trying to find the right words that fit into an appreciated piece of work is more demanding than most people may imagine. However, I have been very lucky and blessed to find many people that have helped me achieve this feat. I would like to take this time to thank them all.

First and foremost, I want to thank Steve Cohen of Macmillan Books for believing in me and encouraging me to hold onto the original manuscript and to tweak it into the book that you are now holding. Steve, for giving me this chance, I will always be grateful. Secondly and with all of my power of appreciation, I thank my executive editor, Marc Resnick of St. Martin's Press for guiding me through this process and making sure that this was going to be a piece of sporting literature that he and I would always be proud to say is ours. Marc, for all of your hard work and giving me this chance, I am extremely grateful. It has been a joy to work with you during this time.

Another big "Thank You" goes out to all of the wonderful touring professionals that provided me with their golden nuggets of mental mistakes. For opening up and giving me their time and insights, I wish to thank: Walter Zembriski, Larry Nelson, Bob Charles, Raymond Floyd, Nick Price, Robert Floyd, Charles Howell III, Greg Norman, David Charles, Jim Thorpe, Jan Stephenson, Bobby Collins, Dick Mast, Mike Hulbert, Patrick Damron, Robert Damron, Per-Ulrik Johanson, Grier Jones, Nick Dougherty, Kelly Froelich, Denis Watson, Wayne Grady, Cameron Yancey, Richie Ramsay, Deanne Pappas, Jessica Schneider, Jan Meierling, Brad Bryant, Mark McNulty, Andy Bean, Aaron Wright, Marc France, Ashley Prange, Julieta Granada, Jonathan Moore, Drew Weaver, Karin Sjodin, Mark Lye, , Rick Rhoden, Seol-An Jeon, Perry Swenson, Hugh Biaocchi, D. A. Points, Jeehae Lee, Naree Song, Suzann Pettersen, Sandra Gal, Bob Lohr, Jhared Hack, Maria Hjorth, Michelle Wie, Laura Baugh, Steven Reed, Justin Rose, and Brian Davis.

Also a great note of appreciation goes out to some of the greatest teachers in the world who every day face the mayhem of emotionally and psychologically challenged golfers. Most notably of these is my good friend David Leadbetter and my colleagues at the Leadbetter Golf Academy: Sean Hogan, Kevin Smeltz, Ron Grotjan, Matt Hilton, and Jodi Hitchcock. Also thanks to wonderful coaches, teachers and amateur golfers such as Mark Guhne, Danny Yoon, Dave Jones, Jim Mitus, Darin Tennyson, Christine Suchy, Ornelle Nouveau, Alicia Stauffacher, Kali Griggs, Ramsay Quinn, Doug Smith, Brandon Eberle, Scott Walsh, and Steven Enfanto. Without your help and insights, none of this would have been possible. I thank all of you for your openness and consideration to make this work a true joy to complete!

Also, I would like to thank esteemed golfers Dr. Robert Wharen, Dr. Joseph Diliberto, Richard Fosler, Granger Beaton, John Hughes, Joanne Martorana, and Rich Smith for taking the time to read earlier manuscripts and provide valuable feedback. I appreciate your insights and golfing acumen into developing a wonderful final work.

A big note of thanks goes out to my longtime good friend, Rich Lerner, who read a version of an earlier manuscript and was kind enough to write my foreword. Rich always has a way to speak the right words and also has a special talent for putting his thoughts on paper with eloquence and simplicity. Thank you Rich for all of your support and for introducing me to some special people along the way!

To my lovely wife, April, I thank you for all of your wonderful support and for always being there when I needed an ear to listen to how things were progressing. Your feedback is always honest, warm, and thought provoking.

Finally, I want to thank you for picking up this book and reading it. After all, this book was written for you. It is my great hope that you find this information helpful as you eliminate your mental errors and enjoy unbelievable success on the links!

INDEX